Out of Darkness into Light
My Personal Journey Into the Realm of Spirit
Foreword by John Edward

LYDIA CLAR

Out of Darkness into Light
My Personal Journey Into the Realm of Spirit

Foreword by John Edward

iUniverse, Inc.
New York   Bloomington

Out of Darkness into Light: My Personal Journey Into the Realm of Spirit

Copyright © 2009 by Lydia Clar

All rights reserved. No part of this book may be used or reproduced by any means, graphic, electronic, or mechanical, including photocopying, recording, taping or by any information storage retrieval system without the written permission of the publisher except in the case of brief quotations embodied in critical articles and reviews.

iUniverse books may be ordered through booksellers or by contacting:

iUniverse
1663 Liberty Drive
Bloomington, IN 47403
www.iuniverse.com
1-800-Authors (1-800-288-4677)

Because of the dynamic nature of the Internet, any Web addresses or links contained in this book may have changed since publication and may no longer be valid. The views expressed in this work are solely those of the author and do not necessarily reflect the views of the publisher, and the publisher hereby disclaims any responsibility for them.

ISBN: 978-1-4401-4777-7 (sc)
ISBN: 978-1-4401-4778-4 (ebook)

Printed in the United States of America

iUniverse rev. date: 06/15/2009

ACKNOWLEDGEMENTS

I want to thank Helene, Joe and Kim, Daria, Irene, Debra, Nancy, Sandy, Mark, Yo, Lucy, Janet, Cathy, Dina, Bettina, Sophie, Marcia, and Carla who have contributed their personal experiences as validation to my work.

Those that I have worked with throughout the years know that I don't remember what I say after a reading. In going over your individual validations for this book, I was humbled by your comments. My thanks cannot convey my gratitude and I send a prayer that God may continue to bless all of you,

To those who throughout my career have generously written to me expressing gratitude for a reading or a class experience, remember that in joining energies during those readings or class experiences, you have enriched my life as well. Thank you!

Blessings to all of you,
Lydia

Following is a prayer you might recite on a daily basis.

PRAYER FOR LIGHT
O God of love
The Peace of Heaven is your gift.
Grant peace and light to all who have journeyed on.
Free them from any anxieties and give understanding to those of us left behind.
Help us to become beacons of light that will spread rays of your love and peace on earth.
Enlighten us to be clean of mind and spirit so that we may fulfill your desires for the spiritual enlightenment of those on earth.
Make us one with You in love forever.
AMEN

This book is dedicated to the memory of William A. Colon, Jr. who was a great part of my life and of this book. His contribution, before his passing, to its creation was instrumental in its being published today. Thank you Bill, although you are gone, I know you are close.

FOREWORD
BY JOHN EDWARD

LYDIA CLAR

Dictionary.com defines the word "journey" as:

A passage or progress from one stage to another.

Your journey of spiritual development might be leading you to pick up this book and to absorb its content.

For years, I have known that when the student is ready the teacher appears. I believe, however, it goes much deeper than that. When you are ready to make a change in your life and make an active decision to do so, I believe that the Universe will conspire to assist you. If so, then how can you ignore a personal Universal opportunity for growth?

Writing the foreword to this book has forced me to sit back and re-examine my own journey and to further expand it to its present progression.

At 15 years of age, speaking to the dead, writing books, hosting television shows and conducting world tours all dealing with the Other Side, (talking to dead people basically), was not what I or any of my contemporaries were interested in as a career choice. Nor, do I remember them being interested in spirit guidance from the great beyond unless it was going to assist them on the SAT scores.

Though all the normal issues that concerned me at the time were front and center, there was always something else. They were ever-growing questions "Is this all I am" and "Is this what my life is supposed to be like?"

No doubt that if this book is in your hands and you are reading my words it's because your higher self, your guides, your dead relatives guiding you, God... or all of the above, are giving you the chance to actually answer those questions for yourself.

LYDIA CLAR, who wrote "Out of Darkness Into Light", was the spokesperson for me at that age. She was guided into my life at a crucial point to spark and ignite that aspect of who I am. She didn't do it for me. I remember clearly calling her and asking her to 'tell me what to do". Her quick and succinct response was, "I cannot". I remember feeling like "you can't push me down the Rabbit Hole and not come on the journey with me." She did, however, send me my first box of "business cards". Looking back, a quarter of a century later, I understand what she meant.

You see, I truly wasn't asking her for guidance, I was asking her "to do it for me". It is no different from someone who is out of shape and overweight, talking to a fitness expert about health and wellness, and ordering the latest piece of exercise equipment from TV. The bottom line is, if you are not the one USING it and DOING it, your body doesn't change. So, yes, YOU need to take in the information in this book, and actually apply it to yourself.

Our journey is just that... Our Own... but it's interconnected and collective just like threads that are woven together to form a blanket. Each thread needs to be strong and fortified in order to sustain the creation of the beautiful blanket; otherwise, it frays and falls apart.

Ask yourself the question. "Why are you holding or reading this book?" Are you embarking on a professional career decision, do you have questions on different issues and relationships, are you trying to break free of all the programming that your family and society has downloaded upon you, do you feel depressed and wonder if there is more to you and your purpose? I have no doubt whatsoever that you are answering yes to most of these questions on some level.

Lydia is a great teacher and communicator of metaphysical principles and teachings. She will inspire you to achieve your personal best and to learn the life lessons to enrich your soul.

Enjoy the journey it's yours after all

John Edward

CONTENTS

INTRODUCTION

This book is written to help the reader gain awareness of self and others. It gives an overview of my own spiritual journey with the hope that it will stimulate the reader's imagination and nurture an interest to develop their own spiritual natures. Development through exploration of the many and diverse areas of parapsychology opens doors to learning. It points out first who you are and second what you'd like to do with the knowledge.

Expansion of self awareness (and your own talent) creates a place where you can better understand yourself and those around you. By recognizing your talents, you will also learn to recognize and accept your neighbor's.

Throughout the ages, mankind has produced talented people whose works in science, philosophy, and the arts, have advanced knowledge, enhanced understanding, and elevated our ability to get more out of life. The progress achieved by each generation is best measured by the talents it recognizes and encourages in others.

Talent requires study, determination and sharing. These three aspects of development, along with the perspective that comes from the responses of others ultimately become one's own experience. Of course, the true value of talent can only be realized if its achievements are known. Talent sets standards and opens the mind to new possibilities by demonstrating that the boundaries of the attainable are determined only by human imagination. In the final analysis that's why it is important for those who do not believe they have a natural ability and who have to work doubly hard to perform well, be provided with examples

The reward of talent lies in the using and sharing of the gift. We seem to have forgotten that and tend to glorify only the accomplishment. In doing so, we have devalued its importance. The world would be a sadder and more ignorant place if the great scientific and artistic minds had not shared the product of their talents.

On a smaller scale, we would be equally unfortunate if individuals were not to share their own personal gifts with one another or, were to withhold their talents in anticipation of some tangible reward.

It is easy to recognize the talent of a great scientist or artist. It is not easy to recognize, the talent of the individual who contributes to the lives of others by sharing a natural gift in everyday life. Too many people tend to see the rich and famous reap their public rewards and to assume that their own special gifts are of less value.

What are these individual talents that can make a difference in the lives of others? One is the gift of understanding, the ability to listen and perceive; Another is the gift for insight, the ability to discard the insignificant and recognize the essential, and yet another is the gift of intuition, the ability to discover an answer among apparently unrelated questions. Whether those talents are defined as the ability to sympathize or to organize, they are as vital to human relationships as the talents of the scientist or artist. On both levels, the universal and personal, talent is creative and must be shared in order to have meaning as well as value.

In our personel lives, worth can only be measured by answering two questions:

1. Did we develop our own talent to the utmost?
2. Was our talent shared with others?

In the end, the answer to both questions must be "yes", because it is only through sharing that a person's ability can be transformed from a possession to a gift.

It is in keeping with this thought and in the spirit of sharing that I present the following pages. I cannot say that I have used my talent to the utmost, for I hope that I will continue to broaden its use throughout the days of my life -- Growth, a process, a way, not an end. When my time comes to leave this dimension behind, I hope I can look back and say, I did it!

SELF AND SPIRIT

Everyone's progress towards enlightenment lies in his or her own hands. We receive according to our own will and capacity to do so. Integral to that progress is the need to learn and interpret the relationship between the psychic and physical aspects of our nature. One without the other is severely limited. In balance and harmony, they awaken our spiritual selves and enable us to receive messages being transmitted from all around and above us. In reflecting upon my life, I can say that I have gone from one miracle to another. Spirit has always watched over me and stepped in at various stages of my development to either save my life (so that I could continue), or introduce people into it that would put me onto the next level of my spiritual pathway.

Perhaps my own experience will help you.

When I was a child I was considered bright and funny. Fact was I didn't consider most of what I did as anything but ordinary. I played like other kids, sometimes alone and sometimes with friends, but the majority of my childhood was spent around adults. My home was the focal point for most of the members of my family. We lived in a very large apartment in Manhattan, making it possible for all to gather and share. In this environment it was not unusual for the conversation to turn to what today is known as "the occult" and for people to relate their personal experiences.

I heard stories about my maternal grandmother, who died when my mother was nine years old. She was acknowledged as being a very gifted medium and healer. Everyone, without exception, spoke respectfully of her power for healing and of her good work for the poor. Born in Puerto Rico to a Spanish family and a life of wealth, she was later disinherited by her family for marrying my grandfather (also from Spain), but whom her family judged to be beneath her station in life. Despite her lack of funds, she continued to care for the poor and sick with whatever means available to her. She gave birth to three children and died by the age of 32.

My mother grew up under very difficult circumstances. My grandfather remarried and more children were born. As the oldest, my mother started to work at a very early age in order to help the family. At the age of 21 she moved to New York City. On arrival, she got a job in the city's teeming west side garment district. She worked there, progressing in her position, for nearly 50 years until shortly before her death. I still have copies of articles written about her in WOMEN'S WEAR DAILY

In a way, my mother's life might be said to have been an example of the best, if less glamorous side, of the women's movement. She could not be described as a feminist and probably would have dismissed any suggestion that she was. Yet, she embodied what I like to think of as the essence of feminism. Not merely because she moved to New York alone at a time when young women were expected to remain at home waiting for a husband; but because of what she was in good times and bad. She was, brave, strong, self-reliant, constant, resourceful, positive, and, above all, loving. My father, whom she met In Puerto Rico, followed her shortly thereafter and they were married in New York City. From her earnings, she would send money home and continued to help support her family. Later, some of them also moved to New York. My exposure to all the family and friends helped to shape my life.

Somehow, I became the unofficial family guide. At the age of nine I was leading people through the mysteries of the New York Transit System. When I was ten I was allowed to travel unaccompanied from Manhattan to New Jersey to visit one of my aunts. This entailed taking the subway to the Port Authority Bus Terminal and then riding a bus through the Lincoln Tunnel and on to Jersey City, a trip of less than 10 miles and well over an hour. I mention this only to indicate that from an early age I was regarded and treated more as an adult than as a child. No one ever said anything to that effect and I certainly never gave it much thought. That simply was the way of it.

As very young children, my brother and I shared a bedroom and one night when I was about five or six years old, I had a dream and was so scared that I started to cry and scream. My mother came running to see what was wrong. She was afraid that, in addition to finding something wrong with me, I would wake my brother up. She asked what was wrong and I told her about my dream. I explained that I had seen myself asleep in my bed, that I had heard someone knock on the front door and saw my mother open it to some men dressed like soldiers. They, in turn had come down the hall carrying a coffin and deposited it at the foot of my bed. After a while my mother succeeded in calming me down and I went back to sleep. The night had come, but it was not over.

Some time later we were all awakened. This time there WAS someone at the front door and the doorbell was ringing insistently. It was a distant cousin of my mother's, who lived in the building next to us, and who was crying hysterically. Through her sobs she told us that she had received notification that her brother, who was in the military service, had been killed. Now there was weeping all around and I grew cold with fear as my mind made an instant connection between my dream earlier that same night and this sad, sudden and undeniable reality.

What I could not have possibly known then and learned only much later was that I was already undergoing the process of spiritual development. No one knew, least of all me. In fact, that traumatic experience caused me to develop a mental block against anything that had to do with the psychic. As I mentioned previously, psychic ability and knowledge of psychic phenomena were present in my formative years.

My mother used to tell a story of how shortly after my birth, I developed a case of dysentery that no doctor could cure. They expected me to die of dehydration. My paternal grandmother told my mother of an old man, an herbalist named Don Bernardo, who lived in the Puerto Rican countryside. As a last resort, they took me to him. The man, according to my mother, was a gifted healer. He told my mother that I had been given "the evil eye" and that I was close to dying. He gave my mother a remedy made from herbs for me. My mother did not know what the herbs were, just that they saved my life. Today herbal remedies are considered part of Homeopathy and its effectiveness is once again being recognized and becoming wide spread.

This was just one of the many stories, associated with the supernatural, concerning me that I heard as I was growing up. Combined with my dream experience, it had a decidedly negative effect. I was frightened. I chose the only defense that, in my child's mind, was available to me. I created a mental wall between my physical and my spiritual selves. I stopped dreaming!

When I was about 7 years old, my parents were divorced and later my mother re-married. I missed my Dad, but at an early age I learned that I had to go on with what life dealt me. I actually got along well with my stepfather. About three years later, when I was ten years old, I decided, out of the clear blue, that I wanted to go to boarding school. I was sent to St. Clare's Academy, in Hastings-on the Hudson, New York. My brother had been attending the same boarding school for about two years. The years that I attended St. Clare's proved to be years of spiritual renewal for me. They gave me peace and at the same time helped me to interact with people of my own age and to understand life at their level. It also helped me to understand and develop a feeling of greater independence. Additionally, it engendered a feeling for helping students from different parts of the world who were finding it difficult to accept where they were. My exposure to them also created a great desire to travel. My years there were happy ones. I loved the school, but when my brother graduated and was going to another High School, I again made the decision that I would also leave and return home. As I mentioned before, I made the decisions, and, ironically, no one questioned them. I was treated as an adult. Thinking back on it, I am amazed and don't rightly know how I would react today, if I was the parent.

My mother moved us to East Elmhurst in Queens, New York so that we could be in a more suburban environment. My brother went to Newtown High School and I went to the local parochial school, St. Gabriel's in East Elmhurst, from which I graduated from the eighth grade. I remember how scared I was during that year about graduating and taking the New York State Regents exams. The class was sent to The Blessed Sacrament School in Jackson Heights to take the tests. I was taking exams that would be comparable to the SAT's today, in a strange school and a nervous wreck. Math was not my strong suit. I remember going over the test and not knowing (probably my fear blocking me) how to work out the problems. I also remember putting my pencil down, bowing my head and saying a Hail Mary, and asking for help. My faith in the Virgin Mary was strong even as a child. I picked up my pencil, started to read the problems again and it became so easy, I didn't even know what was happening. I had turned into this math wiz and just decided to plow through and the heck with it. I finished among the first few and when my papers were picked up I was allowed to leave. That's when realization hit. I had finished. I did very well in that exam as well as the other Regents Exams I had to take. Who helped me? Was it my faith that someone was there to help me, or just the subconscious realization that I could do it? I think it was both. In the long run, passing gave me confidence at a very young age that I could accomplish whatever I set my mind to.

At about fifteen years old my block, the "non-dream" period (and the wall I had subconsciously created), started to crumble. My mother was in a terrible financial situation. My stepfather was very ill in the hospital and the medical bills, as well as our daily living expenses, were mounting. My mother was doing her best to support us but it simply was not enough. She did not know where to turn.

By that time, I was also attending Newton High School. The school was so crowded that classes were split into two sessions so that renovations could be done. I was assigned to the afternoon session which allowed me to sleep later in the morning. Usually, I was alone with our enormous German shepherd dog "Baron". One morning, after my mother left for work and my brother to school, I dreamed for the first time that I could remember. In the dream a deceased friend of my mother's appeared in my bedroom doorway and said, "You'd better get up or you'll be late. It's 6:25." I looked at the clock and it was about 10:00a.m. I thought to myself "that doesn't make any sense, it's not 6:25." Suddenly my bed was shaking so violently that I was thrown to the floor. My first thought was "earthquake" or that Baron had jumped on my bed and accidentally knocked me off. However, there was no quake and the dog was nowhere to be seen. Yet, there I was on the floor, half asleep and confused. Something prompted me to go to the telephone and call my mother. She asked me why I was calling. I said I just knew I had to and recounted the dream. She answered in a calm and normal tone that it was okay. That seemed odd but feeling reassured and still half asleep, I went back to bed and gave the incident no more thought.

That night, my mother was clearly excited when she arrived home. She asked me to repeat my dream to her in detail. I explained whatever parts I still remembered. Suddenly it dawned on me that, for the first time in many years, I had had a dream. Before I could think about it any further, my mother handed me $50. She explained that after my call she kept thinking about the dream and that around lunchtime she went over to a friend at work. There was a man visiting and she told them both about the call. The man said "I would play that 625 number if I were you. If you'd like I'll take care of it for you." She did. She handed over all of her lunch money and at the end of the day, she had won. She was able to pay off her bills and give me the $50 so that I could buy something new to wear for Easter. I was amazed that my mother had listened to me since at that point I didn't even remember exactly what I had said. Nonetheless, I was very grateful because without those $50 I was going to be the only one of my friends with nothing new to wear at Easter. "Spirit" was taking care of me even then. That Easter became another spiritual turning point for me.

My curiosity into the spirit world was re-awakened. I started to take notice of the different ways in which I was helped. It also brought to mind, that once I made up my mind to do something, the way was opened for me – like magic.

MESSAGES

When I was 18, my mother took me to get my first reading. We visited a man named John who worked in a tea room close to where she worked in New York City. He was a slightly flamboyant, show business type who did card readings to supplement his income as an actor. He was also very prophetic. He told me that he saw a blond boy around me and that the child would have a great impact on my life. At that point I wasn't married and thought how wonderful the future was going to be. Little did I know that this man's reading would be yet another turning point later on in my life.

Soon after that, my dreams intensified. I was able to identify aspects of my everyday life --family, work, friends-- through dreams. Sometimes, however, the dreams were just plain unintelligible. I was dreaming in full color and in detail, but there were symbols I still could not interpret. I regarded them with a shrug and gave them little or no thought.

By the age of 19, other changes occurred. I married Bill and the "dream dam" broke, the flow was prodigious, even though I did not take them all that seriously. A strange incident happened shortly after I was married. It was the Christmas season and I had a dream that I entered my living room and my husband and mother were trying to hide something. I went straight to a desk and started to type. In the dream l saw and heard myself typing and typing. I awoke with a very pleasant, satisfied feeling. The next morning I mentioned it to my husband who shook his head and laughed. He called my mother and they shared this big joke. I started to get annoyed because I didn't know what the joke was but felt it was directed at me. He then told me, "I just bought you a typewriter for Christmas and took it to your mother's house to hide it so that it would be a surprise." I think they were more surprised than I.

On the occasion of my 25th birthday, I dreamed that I was wearing a string of long, beautiful pearls. When I awoke on the morning of my birthday, I rationalized my dream by associating the pearls with my birthstone for the month of June. A couple of hours later, my mother visited and brought me a present of a beautiful double string pearl necklace.

Later I came to understand that the whys and wherefores of these dreams were of relatively minor importance. What mattered was that they were pre-cognitive dreams. At first, and for the most part, they were anecdotal and often humorous. As I became more accustomed to and relaxed in my dreams, they became more and more relevant to my life and my very existence.

Once the dreams became second nature to me, I began to wonder what else there was or if they were merely a point of contact for something else. I believed I was ready to learn and move ahead, but development comes slowly and in bits and pieces, one step at a time. I had overcome what for me had been a personal barrier and was dreaming regularly at that point. Consciously and sub-consciously, I was asking some rather heavy questions. What else is there? Why am I here? Who am I, really? What am I supposed to do with what I have.

I mentioned earlier that development comes slowly, which is probably for the best because it helps us understand and assimilate our talents in a more enlightened way.

My mother had a friend, Doňa Maria Koch, who was a very gifted medium. Doňa Maria was not only extremely gifted, but humble and simple in her way of being. One day I found out that she did readings for friends and asked her to do one for me. She did. Her reading was insightful and her predictions came through one after the other. The lady has now passed on but I still think of her often. I became intrigued by her readings. It triggered a feeling that I wanted to know the HOW of it.

Bill and I lived in Forest Hills, New York and had been married a while. I was working in an office with some people who were also interested in the subject of psychic phenomena. It was no accident that we met as we did. We were on different paths toward higher levels of psychic development, yet each of us was directly or indirectly, instrumental in the development of the others.

One day we heard about Reverend Buelah Brown, who ran a spiritual church on the west side of Manhattan. My co-workers and I invited my mother to come along and the four of us went for readings. I will always remember how shocked I was when I entered the office where Reverend Brown did her readings. As I walked in she said to me, "My dear, my dear, what has happened to you? You were meant to be a famous actress. You would have been a star!" Up to that point, I had never revealed to anyone outside the family, that I had wanted to be a dancer on Broadway. I loved all those musicals.

No doubt that this particular ambition is commonplace among young girls, but I truly loved to dance. My mother, however, took the position that dancing was not a career I should look into. In those days, and particularly in the Latin culture, there was no such thing as rebellion, so I set my ambition aside. Yet, so many years later, here was a woman that I didn't know, repeating the sentiments as if she had been present when the discussion took place all those years ago. I just sat there and stared at this insightful woman, reliving a painful memory. There was more to the moment than a recollection. She was fanning a creative spark in me, and reaching a part of me that I thought was long dead. I felt as if she understood it as no one else had.

As a child, I had demonstrated a talent for the dance and, more importantly, had experienced the joy of it in dance and piano classes provided for me "by my aunt Lydia". My other aunt Josephine, who still lives in New Jersey, also loved to dance and taught me more. It was fun but I also know that she appreciated my ability and derived great pleasure from helping me take it further. I still love to dance. That day, sitting in Reverend Brown's office, all I could think to answer was "My mother wouldn't let me!" Reverend Brown just stared at me for what seemed like a long time. Then she resumed and went on to tell me many fascinating things, but the one that made the most lasting impression was the first. How could she know or intuit all that? Naturally, my curiosity increased. I started reading all the books on the subject I could get my hands on. My friends and I would borrow a book at the library, or buy one, read it and pass it on in order to save money. There were many books and readings after that

MRS. ENA TWIGG!-
AND MY EXPOSURE
TO PSYCHOMETRY

Several years later, my co-worker and friend, Roz Safrin, (now deceased and communicating with me in other ways), decided to go to London. We had read a book in which the famed British psychic, Ena Twigg was mentioned. We thought it would be wonderful if during our visit to London we could arrange a meeting with her. The company for which we worked in New York had an office in London and we asked one of our New York senior executives, who was also interested in the psychic field, to call the head of the London office and ask him to set up an appointment for us. Needless to say, he wasn't too thrilled with the idea, fearing that the British manager might ridicule him. However, being more curious than apprehensive, he agreed to do it. The British manager accepted the request without comment or qualms and when we reached London our appointments had already been set up.

The only stipulation was that we call Mrs. Twigg when we arrived at the hotel to confirm the appointment. We debated as to who would call her as we both felt a bit odd about just calling and saying, "hi, we're here." Roz finally called and chatted away on the phone with Mrs. Twigg. She said to Roz: "Your mother is here (Roz's mother had passed on years before) and she is telling me that there's something wrong with your leg." Hearing only one side of the conversation, I thought it odd when Roz said, "There's nothing wrong with my leg". They chatted for another few minutes and the appointments were confirmed for the next day. When Roz got off the phone I asked her what the statement was about and she explained that Mrs. Twigg had said there was something wrong with her leg. "But there's nothing wrong with either of my legs," Roz said. As she walked towards the bathroom, I looked in her direction and let out a shout. "Roz, what's wrong with your leg?" Her foot was bleeding. It was nothing serious, just blood from a burst blister caused by the new shoes she had travelled with . We were, none the less, speechless. The looks on our faces said it all.

Ena Twigg's home was in the quiet residential neighborhood of East Acton, a suburb of London. It was away from the commotion and noise of the West End. She and her husband greeted us warmly. As we chatted she seemed every bit the charming, lady one might see in a British film. She asked us if we had something that she could hold onto during the reading. She explained about psychometry and that she would use the object while working. We both said that we would find something for her to hold. Each reading was private and when she began she became serene and highly focused. When my turn came, I handed her a small gold and pearl pin I was wearing and she proceeded to tell me the origin of the pin and went right on reading me. This was another first for me. I'd never seen psychometry used before and was fascinated as Mrs. Twigg zeroed in on me by holding that little pin.

One of the things she mentioned was that I should be careful around water. That I would be saved three times and that it might not be possible after that. She was right. The first time was when I was a child of about eight or nine years old. My aunt Ana had taken me to Jones Beach on Long Island. The surf was high that day, but I was a pretty good swimmer and was jumping or ducking under the waves. Suddenly two waves came in succession and I didn't see the second one which knocked me under. I could feel the undertow dragging me into deep water. I fought desperately, but the force of the current was too great. I had swallowed some water and my lungs felt as if they were about to burst. Oddly, I could see myself struggling; then a feeling of intense peace came over me and I started to pray. I knew it was the end. Right after that, another current grabbed me, dragged me along the bottom in another direction, and tossed me onto the beach. I was scratched from head to toe and bleeding, but I had been saved. This was during the period I was blocking my psychic abilities so I didn't acknowledge anything except to thank God for having saved me.

The second time was around the age of eleven when I was in boarding school in Hastings-on-the Hudson, north of the New York City in Westchester County. The nuns had taken us swimming in the nearby Saw Mill River Creek. The water was barely knee deep, so I felt no need to be particularly careful as I waded around looking for fish and enjoying this refreshing break from the heat of the day. Suddenly it was as if the bottom had gone out from under me. I had tumbled into a natural hole in the streambed and it was as if, I was being pulled in. I struggled, managed to right myself and get back to the surface. I emerged gasping for air and quickly realized that no one had noticed what had happened to me. After all, the water was knee deep. How could anyone drown?

The third time (although for purposes of the book I am projecting ahead in time) was when I was much older and living back in Manhattan. I decided to take a cruise to the Bahamas. It was a brand new ship on its maiden voyage. The ship departed from the port of Miami, FL. On the first night out, I detected the odor of smoke, the kind usually produced by an electrical fire. It bothered me for three days. I mentioned it to a steward and my cabin was checked. They found nothing. I spoke to several people and they told me they smelled nothing. But it was only a three-day trip out of Florida and I didn't have to live with it for very long. Back in Miami I felt a bit ridiculous, because nothing had happened.

Nevertheless, I was glad to be off the ship, which was scheduled for a brief visit to a shipyard in New Orleans. It was to be checked over after its first voyage for whatever startup problems were present. It left Miami the following day, but never arrived at its destination. According to the report on the front page of *The New York Times*, the ship had sunk after being swept by a fire that was believed to have been electrical in origin.

I understood fully what Mrs. Twigg was saying to me about being careful around water. For some reason I started to cry. Perhaps it was because I felt a great sense of relief and discovery all blended into one emotion. Certainly, she had told me nothing devastating or discouraging. Quite the contrary, she had shown me the ways in which I had been helped AND would be helped in the future, because the third episode had not happened yet.

I felt as if I had been led to my psychic source. My mind flashed back over the psychic readings that had affected me so dramatically. In that instant, I decided to really study the phenomenon so that I could understand and use it for the benefit of others. Actually, it was not so much a decision as a realization. I simply knew and accepted that I would try to return, in some measure, what I had received from her on that day.

In a world where materialism and individualism are dominant, there is often no sense of responsibility towards others. Most people do not count their possessions or talents as gifts from God and see no obligation to share with those in need. Yet, we all have a responsibility to share them As Mrs. Twigg shared her talents with me, I was determined to do the same for others.

Shortly after my return from London, Bill and I moved to Upper Montclair, New Jersey . I kept trying to find the right outlet to learn what I felt I needed to know. I started by enrolling in a Yoga course being offered by the local adult education center at the high school in Montclair. This course helped me to recognize the relationship between mind and body and the spirit that joins them. Not long after I completed the class, a new direction opened up for me through the same colleague who had arranged our appointment with Ena Twigg. In casual conversation, he asked me if I would be interested in taking a course in numerology which was being offered at his son's nursery school.

I realized instantly that I was being given the opportunity to study another area of the psychic realm. The course was taught by another British medium, Dr. Alfreda Oliver, founder and director of the Transcendental Psychic Arts School. What I learned was how to interpret the mystery of numbers and an individual's life patterns, through the soul quality, personality, life and Karmic lessons. I also learned how to create a chart, expressing the meaning of the individual numbers and patterns created from a person's name and date of birth as it appears on the birth certificate.

Many years later, while living in Manhattan, I again took another numerology class taught by Ellen Dodge-Young (Now Ellen Dodge living in Arizona.)

Upon completion of the Numerology course with Dr. Oliver, I went on to study the tarot in another of Dr. Oliver's classes. Her method was as unconventional as it was creative. She taught the tarot, card by card, and required her students to color each card in order to memorize every detail. I confess that I soon became bored. The tarot was fascinating, but the course was just going too slowly for me. I didn't want to seem presumptuous, but the fact was that I felt like a graduate student in a freshman course which was, of course, ridiculous as I had never studied the tarot before. However, I knew I had to move on and left the class and began teaching myself how to read with a plain deck of cards.

I practiced on friends and co-workers. Their reactions were most encouraging. They would say, "pretty good" or "not bad" and, at that point, it was as if they were saying "great." I found it hard to believe that the information I was giving out was correct, but I couldn't contradict their feedback. At that time I thought back to something Dr. Oliver had said to me when I left her Tarot Class. "One day you will be doing what I'm doing and you will be telling other people about themselves". I had thanked her and thought, Lord, I hope so. Now, so many years later, I understood what she meant and she was proved right!

I cite these personal experiences to make the point that everyone we meet along our spiritual life path is there for a reason and as part of our souls' evolution. They may be imparting a message or a lesson. It is up to us to determine which. The same may be said about the people and situations we encounter in our daily lives.

THE HEALING ARTS

As I moved ahead with my studies and learning, I also continued to commute from New Jersey and hold a regular job in the New York headquarters of a major international public relations firm. By this time, I was Vice President for Administration.

The work was complex and constantly presented me with tight deadlines imposed by perpetually busy and sometimes impatient executives at home and abroad. The pace was fast and the pressure high. I understood that it all came with the territory. I enjoyed my work and valued the friendship of my associates but the long hours spent meeting multiple responsibilities often left me exhausted and tense by the time I arrived home. Worse yet, when recurrent stomach pains sent me to see a doctor, I was diagnosed as having a duodenal ulcer. No one in my family had ever had an ulcer, but there I was, at 31 years of age, sporting one like a business Purple Heart.

Blessings

I remember going to bed that night and feeling extremely low and for some reason, I was also annoyed and asked my spiritual guides "Why has this happened to me?" I fell asleep and started to dream of this beautiful lady, dressed in white. I felt as if I was floating in my dream and I went floating right after her. I realized much later, that I was doing out of body travel. She climbed the stairs in this house and was looking down at me and spit. It landed on my face. I remember that with the spit, I made the sign of the cross and blessed myself. (It reminded me of being in church and the priest using holy water to bless the people). I started to tell my mother, who appeared out of nowhere in my dream, "your mother spit at me, your mother spit at me." My mother looked at me, smiled and said, "she was blessing you"! I awoke feeling very strange.

Naturally, upon awakening, I called my mother and described the dream, leaving out her part in it and emphasizing the spitting incident. In conversation I repeated what I had said to her about her mother spitting at me in the dream. Just as in the dream, her response was, "That means she was blessing you." I almost dropped the phone. As the day wore on, I began to understand that this dream had something to do with the progress of my spiritual development and the ulcer was the pivotal point.

Alternative Healing:

Before I went to sleep, I meditated and prayed that I might be guided to find an answer to my ulcer problem. One night during the late news there was a report about Elizabeth Taylor's health. I became so engrossed in it that I felt as if the face of Elizabeth Taylor was being engraved in my memory for some reason. It was such a strong feeling that I felt as if I had been hypnotized. As soon as the news ended, the sensation ended. It was late and I got ready for bed and went to sleep. I started to dream that I was in a house, looking at a doorway. Before my eyes, a large field of vibrating light started to take form. Anyone who has seen the original Star Trek series on television will know how this white light looked, because it resembled the ionization process depicted whenever the transporter was activated and someone was beamed to another place.

The form started to take the shape of a face. At first, it was the face of Elizabeth Taylor, but then it changed and it wasn't. In the dream I knew that there was a connection to me. The woman asked me if I was all right and if the light was too strong. She said not to get too close to her, because it might harm me. I knew then and there that I was seeing my grandmother again. Except this time, instead of seeing a white shape at a distance, I was seeing her face in detail. I was so excited to understand all of this that I felt a great surge of happiness. She kept asking me if I was all right, but without using words. She was imprinting her messages on my mind telepathically. I was talking, she was not. She said to me "you have to remember this when you wake up". She was talking to me in Spanish and proceeded to give me a remedy for my ulcer. Then she said goodbye. I woke up with a sense of joy.

The next morning I called my mother and after explaining my dream, I asked if she had heard of these ingredients in the recipe my grandmother had given me. Although I remembered what my grandmother had said, I couldn't make sense of it as I didn't really know what they were. My mother said that part of it was sesame seed, but she didn't know the rest. She agreed to call my aunt Lydia to see if she could decipher what it was. She couldn't figure it out either, but said she would ask a religious lady from her church. The woman knew what it was. She explained that the recipe called for sesame seeds liquefied in "magnetized" water". The magnetized water portion was the ingredient my mother, aunt and I couldn't identify. This religious lady told my aunt that she knew what it was and agreed to prepare a bottle of the water for me. The bottle of water was mailed to me and I followed the instructions for taking it. My ulcer healed. Whenever I felt the stress starting I would drink some more and the symptoms would disappear.

Interestingly enough, about 15 years later an article appeared in the "Wall Street Journal" talking about magnets, what they could do and related the story of a company in Wisconsin that claimed that their magnetic device would provide miraculous results if the product was clamped onto a strategic spot like the water pipes in a house to produce softer, magnetized water, OR onto the fuel line of a car to get higher gas mileage, OR yet again, onto a bottle of wine in order to improve the taste.

The Attorney General of the State of Wisconsin, where the product was produced, had filed a suit to "muzzle" the company until it could prove its advertising claims. Today Magnetic products are available on-line and common everywhere.

Acupuncture

This is another ancient form of healing -- at least 4,000 years old - but it has become widely available and popular in the West only within the past 15 or 20 years. Acupuncture originated in the Orient and its principal applications are in pain relief or prevention and in healing. Some medical plans are now reimbursing patients for acupuncture therapy. The procedure itself is pain free and very effective. It consists of placing hair-thin wires on pressure points or along nerve paths in order to block negative impulses to the area. When these wires (they look like very thin needles) are removed, the pressure is removed and the area restores itself.

When I lived in New Jersey and before moving to Florida, I slipped and fell on a patch of ice, which had accumulated after a very heavy snowstorm. As a result of the fall I was diagnosed as having a bulging disk and a herniated disk, which in turn affected the sciatic nerve running from my lower back all the way down my right leg. I was hospitalized for a total of one month, but none of the medications or treatments worked. The pain was as intense as ever.

I was meditating on my condition and asked my guardian angels to help me. I asked that they should bring someone or something to heal me. That same morning a friend from work, called and recommended that I go to a sports medicine/accupuncture doctor who had helped her tremendously. Out of desperation, I called and went to visit this doctor in New York City. I had never had accupuncture before and didn't know what to expect. However, I trusted that I had asked for help and it had been given to me, now it was up to me to follow through.

He was a New York Orthpaedic doctor who specialized in sports medicine. He had gone to Taiwan for training and had learned the procedures from a Chinese doctor. On my first visit I practically crawled into his office and after the first treatment I walked out under my own steam. Although I still had pain, I could bear it and concentrate on using my own healing forces to recuperate totally. Without exaggeration, after being set free of the terrible pains that had tortured me for so long, I felt as if I had experienced another miracle..

My situation exemplifies but one of the many uses of acupuncture. I have read that in China and Cuba it is used in place of anesthetics during surgery and childbirth. Among its advantages is that it has no side effects like traditional anesthesia. It is certainly less expensive.

NEXT STEPS

I credit my grandmother, even though she passed when my mother was 9 years old, as being instrumental in the continuance of my spiritual journey. It had been quite a while since I'd had my first dream with her and I didn't know it then, but my journey was about to undergo another progressive modification.

One night, I went to bed feeling unusually sad and depressed; so much so that I started to cry without knowing why. I fell asleep and I began to dream that I was with my grandmother. I was seated at a dining table and she served me something to eat that was like a dessert. It was very sweet and I kept thinking I wasn't going to be able to finish it. I didn't want to offend her and when she asked me if I liked it, said, "oh yes, it's delicious." She smiled and was pleased. Then she told me it was time I had a master teacher and that she had selected one for me. She herself couldn't stay, but my teacher, whom she called *Yaffo*, would stay with me always. She kept repeating and repeating the name and stressing that I had to remember the name because I should call on him whenever I needed help. I was very upset because she was leaving. She told me not to cry and to remember the name *Yaffo*. Then she was gone. I woke up repeating the name to myself.

I carried this upset feeling for a couple of days, but soon realized I was being prepared for something else. I just didn't know what.

I continued with my work and my classes. Then, a couple of months later, I had another dream. It was as if I had been waiting for it. I saw myself asleep in bed, but yet I felt awake. My attention was being attracted to a movement above me to my right, to where the ceiling met the outer wall. Penetrating the wall was the most intense white light I had ever seen. I looked at it for as long as I could and then was forced to close my eyes because the light was blinding me. I knew this was a manifestation of God. I felt intense love and release while at the same time a great fear of the power over me.

The light covered me completely and intensified. Next I felt a hand pull off what I thought was some skin from my eyes and I heard 'a voice say, "Now you will be able to see." I was overwhelmed and so frightened I wouldn't open my eyes. Yet, I knew instinctively that no harm would come to me.

When I awoke I felt a great sense of peace. As I think back on this incident, what stays with me is that in the nights that followed this dream, I would close my eyes in the darkness and laugh to myself because I was seeing. At first I would see the entire bedroom as if it were daytime. Then, still awake, but with my eyes closed, I would see images and people. I enjoyed these interludes so much that I didn't realize how much or what it signified. Up to that point, I had been able to see only in a dream state. Now I was seeing while fully awake. I'm embarrassed to say that, initially, I played with it and enjoyed myself tremendously with my new gift.

Not long after that I reached another turning point in my personal life. I felt that I needed change. I didn't really know what it was that kept pushing at me, other than the knowledge that I needed to make a change. One night I went to sleep and I was rather restless. I remember having a feeling of anticipation that made it hard for me to sleep. When I finally did sleep, I dreamed that I was in a great arena-style auditorium. Everything was white -- the walls, seats, and the clothing of all of the people who filled the auditorium. Suddenly a roar went up from the audience and everyone stood up and started to clap. I was impressed and curious so I stood up to see what it was all about and who it was that was being so enthusiastically received. To my amazement, the object of this reception headed right towards me. I realized it was a cousin of my mother's, Nati, who had passed on many, many years before.

As a child I was extremely fond of her and was fascinated by the talking parrot she kept at home. I always looked forward to Nati's visits, because she always brought me something, usually candy. On one occasion, she brought me a huge plastic pencil that contained a dozen regular pencils inside. The pencils were printed with my deceased grandmother's name.

She explained that when she was having them engraved for me, the only name that came to her was my grandmother's. In my dream, I realized that my grandmother had always been with me and was, even now, trying to reach me through Nati. I kept those pencils for many, many years. I hadn't thought about them in quite a while and it was only as I was writing this book so many years later, that I recognize the symbolism of the pencils. At that point (and at a very young age for me) she was telling me I would write.

To this day I recall vividly, and with love, the picnics Nati would take me on with her niece and her niece's children. I still look through the pictures taken back then which Nati had given me, for the future.

Therefore, when in my dream I realized who it was, I ran towards her. In the process, people were trying to keep me from reaching her. She was such a highly evolved soul that it was just not proper for me to go near her. She smiled at me and told the people who were keeping us apart, that it was all right. She had come to see me. I felt so pleased and proud. I was smiling and smiling. Then she said to me "here, we're taking these off of you". I felt my wedding rings being removed from my fingers then she handed them to me. She looked at me again, smiled and, with everyone applauding, left in the direction from which she had come. I woke up with my wedding rings clutched in my hand.

Following this dream, my marital situation changed, not because of the dream but because of the feelings of anxiety that continued within me and which I couldn't explain. I obviously needed to develop my abilities and needed to concentrate on just that. Within a short period of time I moved back home to New York City, where I proceeded to enroll in the Inner vision School, headed by Vera Scott Johnson. Classes were held in a conference room located at the Engineering Center at the United Nations.

The instructor was the Reverend Sophie Bloomfield and my first course outline was called "ESP Development." From day one, the course stressed psychometry. Psychometry was not mentioned in the literature I had received. In retrospect, I am sure that it was no accident. I was meant to start another area of development (or my sense of touch.) The memory of my first encounter with psychometry and my visit with Ena Twigg in London came back to me often during that time. I continued with other courses and teachers in meditation, healing and finally back - to the Tarot.

This time, however, I completed the course and it is the means through which I express my readings today.

At the end of the Inner Vision courses, Mrs. Vera Scott Johnson organized a psychic fair benefiting a charity and I was one of the people selected to do readings.

I went, to the fair full of trepidation. This would be my first public exposure. At the last minute something prompted me to take my regular, plain deck of cards and it was with those that I read the people who came to my table. That raised the eyebrows of the psychic fair's promoters, but they said nothing because I had a very long line of people waiting to be read. It was a very long day and I wasn't able to take even a small break. I worked from the minute I arrived to the very end of the fair. That night I felt very exhilarated and at the same time totally exhausted. I was on a high, albeit tired. Reverend Oliver's (my first teacher) prediction had come true. I was telling other people about themselves.

MEDITATION
& RELIGION

People often ask me How can I develop my spiritual abilities? My stock answer is with a question: Do you meditate? I generally get a no, I'm too busy, I fall asleep, etc. etc." My answer is: If you can't meditate you generally can't develop. Focus has to be learned in order to read effectively. It's a time consuming proposition – one step at a time.

I'd like to start this chapter by saying that meditation is considered non denominational in nature. It has nothing to do with any particular religion, so it can be used by anyone.

In a Miami Herald article entitled Jews Explore Meditation As A Road to Spiritual Depth, the Rabbi explained that many are finding, regardless of their religious affiliation, a deeper connection to God through meditation. The article further offered a very good example to describe the difference between prayer and meditation - - In prayer you speak to God and in meditation you listen.

The above made so much sense to me and cleared my way to returning to Catholicism. I am a Catholic but one, who at that particular time in life, had reached a personal conflict between the teaching of my Catholic faith and the spiritual work I was clearly meant to do. What was right my Catholic upbringing or my spiritual beliefs? It is a conflict that many are facing today. After I read the above mentioned article, I decided that I didn't have to choose. When I go to church now , I can say that I attend mass. I pray, thank and talk to God then I focus my whole being on receiving direction in my life from him directly through a meditative state. It has given me a greater focus on my faith. Prior to that I attended a service that I had been taught by rote and went through by rote. I must say that even though I went through the service by rote, the basic faith instilled in me as a child never left me. I just didn't know how to use it.

Through my moves from New York to Montclair New Jersey and back to New York City, I continued working for the same company, under the same pressure, only worse. It was beginning to get to me. I hadn't done any readings since the fair and I felt as if I was in a state of limbo.

Just then, Janet, a lady whose organization rented space within our offices, came to see me and asked, Have you heard of Silva Mind Control? I told her I hadn't. She explained that it was something she had just heard about and that it was an organization that offered a lecture series on controlling one's own mind in order to alleviate stress and achieve any goals set. She asked me to accompany her to an introductory lecture that week and I did.

It has been said that when the pupil is ready the teacher appears and that was the case for me. At that point in my life I needed a new focus. I was very impressed with the free lecture and signed up for the full weekend package of four consecutive days. The instructor was Paul Grivas, who has now passed on to another life. From Paul I not only learned the Silva Method of concentration and meditation, but also the art of presentation. Paul had a very different way of expressing himself and teaching. He gave examples from his life, his friends and his dog Calhoun. He had a very interesting and funny manner that held everyone's attention. He kept me interested and the course, in turn, helped me to be able to stay focused on my goals. That knowledge enabled me to concentrate more deeply and thus give better readings. My reading methods changed and I felt I had improved a great deal.

Please recall what I said earlier about meeting new people and/or experiencing new situations and the impact that they can have in our lives. Every situation brings a new purpose.

During the Silva course, I had occasion to meet a banker from Philadelphia. We ate lunch together during one of the breaks and I focused closely on what he was saying. Suddenly I started to receive a series of telepathic impressions relating to his work situation and I started to tell him what was happening. He reacted with amazement. He said he was due to give a proposal for a new venture and what I was describing sounded like his business associate and the deal. This presentation was to take place the following week. I described to him a series of events that I was seeing and asked him to follow what I had explained so that his presentation would be successful. When the four-day seminar was over he took my address and promised to let me know what transpired. Two weeks later I received a letter from him. Everything had taken place as I had predicted. He had followed my advice and the project had been approved.

I thanked God and my spiritual guides for the knowledge they had helped me to discover, as well as for enabling me to assist this stranger.

His letter proved important to me as it was the first of the many testimonies and validations I have since received. I realized then that I had reached a milestone in my spiritual progress. For the first time I had given a reading without the help of cards or a psychometric object. My third eye had opened and I could see by concentrating and focusing on a person. I had actually read this man's vibrations, his aura.

Meditation (Four Types)

There are many types of meditation but I consider the following, the primary ones:

1) *Seeking the silence - (transcendental meditation),* In this type you connect with your inner self and become very focused allowing your mind to go blank and into the silence. Buddhist monks, who go into a trance-like state, generally practice this. It is the hardest type of meditation to achieve, because all thought, noise and distractions must be blocked out.

I'd Like to relate an anecdote passed on to me by a friend, Stephen, who lives in Hawaii. He told me about a very spiritual Hawaiian lady who is very much in tune with the ancient Hawaiian religion and mysticism. She is apparently a very giving and sharing person who lives in a house in the country on land that was ceded to her ancestors by King Kamehameha in 1804.

A number of years ago, she and her husband hosted a group of Tibetan Monks who were on some sort of world goodwill tour. Various people were supposed to have sponsored them in their homes, but something happened and because of the mix-up, the organizers of the tour started calling around to see if anyone could take one or two into their homes. This good lady asked how many there were and was told there were ten. She said she would take all ten. She and her husband set up a tent/roof outside, got some beds/futons, erected a little outdoor kitchen and they were all set to receive the monks.

Remember that because of the monk's focus and meditation, their energy is very, very strong. Following are a few of the instances related to me.

a) It seems the monks had never been near the ocean. As a result, when they went in, they tried to breathe under water and almost drowned. They wanted to see what would happen was the explanation that they gave.

b) The neighbors started fighting and screaming and yelling at each other during the entire time the monks were there. Her neighbors had never acted that way before and she and her husband were very embarrassed.

The monks told her that it was a normal occurrence for them and that it happened all the time. It seems that they have so much positive energy that the negative energy nearby gets disturbed and acts up. Wherever they go, the same kind of disturbances happen.

c) When the monks chanted outside, breadfruit, a local Hawaiian fruit, fell off the trees - everywhere but on the monks! They were untouched. She explained that there was an incredible sound to the chant - special spiritual notes. On a visit to this good lady's house, my friend was shown a book of photos from the monks' visit.

The reason I mention this anecdote is to show how meditation, on a positive level, can unsettle or replace the negative, or illness, around a person, place or thing.

2) *Visualization* - This is an easier more active form of meditation because you are mentally viewing a situation while meditating. This is done by going into a meditative state, or within, then visualizing in great detail, whatever you'd like to accomplish. It gives you the freedom to visualize a desire, send healing energy, and increase mental faculties to aid you in achieving whatever you'd like in your life.

3) *Chakra Meditation* - - Chakras are the spiritual centers of the body. There are seven main Chakras on which to meditate. Normally, the meditation is started at base or root chakra ,at the bottom of the spine, and rises to the highest crown chakra, at the top of the head. Each Chakra, or the portion of the body connected to it, has a color associated with it. This color should be used in the meditation process changing the thought and color as you go from one to the other in progression until the meditation is completed. The seven centers are: the base, color red, spleen, color orange, stomach, color yellow, heart,. color green, throat, color sapphire blue, third eye area, *center of the forehead*, magenta color, and the top of the head, the purple color. This is a good technique for healing yourself or someone else as you can concentrate on chakra closest to where the medical problem is.

4) *Inspirational Mediations:* This type of meditation is found in any type of spiritual book, cards or inspirational saying and used as the inspiration for the day, or the food for thought of your spiritual day.

I'd like to quote from a book by Louise L. Hay, titled, Meditations to Heal Your Life In the section on: SPIRITUAL LAWS When I learn the Spiritual Laws of life, 'magic' is demonstrated in my life.

Meditation, has many uses, chief among them is healing. One of the better known uses is for lowering high blood pressure. Let's consider how it works. The mind becomes still and shuts out the causes of tension. The immediate effect is that the body releases trapped tension which in turn allows the heart rate to slow down and lowers the blood pressure. Through this process a person achieves a state of relaxation in which stress is neutralized, (or controlled), allowing the body to use its natural regenerative powers to restore itself.

Today, there are many hospitals, institutions and private practitioners who are employing meditation to heal their patients through the "mind-body-spirit concept"

GUIDING HANDS AND ANGEL PROTECTION

The Silva Mind Control method of meditation opened a new way for me and I no longer felt in limbo. I missed not dreaming with my grandmother, but one night after meditating I found myself in a dream with my mother and my Aunt Lydia. We were walking down a wide boulevard and we saw a large overhead shadow. They looked up, became terrified, and started running into a church. They kept calling me to run and not look up because I would be blinded. I wasn't afraid and calmly looked up to see a huge Angel full of bright white light. He warned me not to look at the light. I answered not to worry, that it wasn't bothering my eyes at all. He smiled at me, said "good". He told me his name was "Curafed". He walked with me in the direction of a church courtyard; reminiscent of the great churches in Europe, with a quadrant in the center with upper and lower levels of columned walkways. When we reached the second level, he handed me a small white square of cloth enclosing something. As he handed it to me he said, Remember, one is for you, and one is for your brother. You have to hold it and return it to him. I agreed. With that, Curafed smiled and flew away. I couldn't contain my curiosity and looked at what was inside. There were two medals of the Virgin Mary. The strange part was that the Virgin was dressed in red and I, to my knowledge at the time, had never seen that anywhere. The Virgins I had seen, were usually clothed in either blue or white. The other question was why two medals?

During mass the following Sunday my mind started to wander. I was looking around the perimeter of the church and, in a side aisle of the very church I had been attending since my move to New York City, was a large, antique wooden statue of the Virgin Mary with a red dress. Again, I had a message and no clue as to what it was. No doubt, 1 was being taught patience and trust. I left it in God's hands to clue me in when the time was right.

A couple of months later, my brother, Juan, who was a career non-commissioned officer in the U.S. Air Force, came home on leave with his family before being shipped to Germany. On the night of their departure, I had a formal dinner to attend at the Waldorf Astoria Hotel and was at home getting dressed when my phone rang. I figured it was my brother. I had promised to drive him and his family to the airport before going to the dinner. My brother's call was to ask me if he could leave his oldest son, Christopher, or Mike as we call him, with me. My brother explained that he believed it was going to be difficult for the boy to get adjusted to living in Germany and that this might hurt his chances of graduating on time from High School and getting accepted into a college. I had loved "Mikey" from the first day 1 set eyes on him in 1962 when I visited my brother during his first tour of duty in Germany. He was also my godson and there was no way I could say no.

It brought back to me the prediction by John, the psychic from the tearoom when I was 18 years old, about the blond boy that I would have in my life. The prediction came to pass all those years later in the form of my nephew. That's why when someone asks me about a time reference during a reading, I always answer that there is no time in space. All 1 can do is *guesstimate* time.

After getting past the initial difficulties that accompanied our new arrangement, Mikey and I both set into a routine of school and work. To my amazement, about three to four months later my other nephew, Mikey's younger brother, Tony, asked if he too could come and live with me. I again said yes and he was sent back from Germany to me. I had the two of them in my, *for two people*, apartment in New York City and we managed.

Tony went away to school for a while but when my brother's tour of duty was up, he returned to the States and Tony went back to live with his father. Mikey, refused to go and stayed with me until he got married. That's when I comprehended the Angel's full message to me, one would stay and one would be cared for and returned to my brother.

Angels were the first messengers sent by God. They are mentioned repeatedly in the Bible and they heralded in a new era when they announced the birth of Christ. We are all taught as children that each of us has a guardian angel. But what is an Angel?

For as long as we know Angels have appeared to mortals, giving them messages, offering protection, and in the end escorting them into Heaven. We think of Angels as beings with large wings, but they take many forms. They can appear as an ordinary person, in order not to frighten the person seeing them, or they can appear in their celestial form. When I saw Curafed in my dream, I saw the celestial form, radiating a great light, as he flew toward me. When he descended and walked next to me into the church courtyard, he behaved like an ordinary individual, with the exception that his wings were down and folded in back of him. The white light he continued to radiate gave off a sense of peace and love.

Many years after my encounter with Curafed, one of the Network magazine shows ran a feature entitled *Angeles – the Mysterious Messengers*. It depicted Angels in all forms and presented people giving testimonies of their encounters with Angels. Some were from near- death experiences, *others in* healings and a variety of other miraculous *earthly* occurrences. It seems that Angels appear in times of need when we are threatened in someway or to announce coming events.

After Mikey (my nephew) married, my friend Shala Mattingly now a master of past life regressions and living in New York City, told me she was doing readings at psychic fairs and asked me if I would be interested in doing the same. She introduced me to the man who was hosting the fairs. I met with him and the interview consisted of my giving him a reading and he in turn giving me one.

He asked me what form my reading would take and I said I would psychometrize something for him. He gave me a ring he was wearing. I gave him a description of a man and his surroundings. I also told him that the man was bent over holding a ring and shaping it with a small hammer. He said that I was correct. The ring had been hand-tooled for him in India. He agreed to let me read at his fairs. I did so on and off for a couple of years and received great exposure. I also did lectures with results similar to those I had when l did my first psychic fair many years before. This continued throughout my association with this fair group. I met many interesting people and made a number of close friends with whom I still have contact.

I remained in New York for about eight or nine years during which, time I suffered some major difficulties in my life, including my mother's illness and death. The need again for a complete change in my life, home, job, and me, in general, came to the fore again. I relocated to New Jersey; this time to North Bergen to give myself a much needed mental and physical rest. I wasn't well and during that time underwent a series of surgeries. Yet, during all that time, the spiritual strength that I had accumulated helped me to overcome some very major obstacles in my life.

God has always watched over me. At the bleakest moments of my life, there was always someone ready to extend a hand from members of my family, who have never let me down, to many good friends and strangers. Somehow, I always managed.

After leaving the psychic fair circuit, I started to do private readings. Some people suggested that I should teach psychic development. I did, but on a private or small group basis, because I wanted to be able to devote more time directly to the individual. My days consisted of holding down a full-time job, teaching the development classes, and doing private readings.

During the years in New York and later on, after my move back to New Jersey, I traveled a great deal. I visited places I never thought I would see. One trip was a-six-week tour of the Orient and India. I regarded this as a particularly important trip because I felt as if I were going on a spiritual journey. I also had other reasons for wanting to go. l would visit my brother in Korea (he was stationed at an air force base outside of Seoul) and I would celebrate my birthday in Nepal. How much more of an exotic place could a person celebrate one's birthday? I was ecstatic.

Two days after booking the trip, I had a dream that I was walking down a street in a foreign city and in the distance I could see something rolling towards me. At first I couldn't figure out what it was. As it got closer I saw that it was a majestic Chinese lady on a rolling vehicle which, to my eyes, consisted entirely of a flat board with what I thought were four wheels. It seemed as if she was floating on air, yet low to the ground. She was sitting in a low position. I couldn't tell if she was sitting on her legs or if she had none. When she reached me she said, The one with the leg problems will be all right. The lady's spiritual strength and aura of authority were palpable. She was dressed in very ornate and richly jeweled oriental clothing (almost like what an Empress would wear) with- a matching crown. She was beautiful. Again the message was transmitted telepathically (her lips didn't move, she just looked straight at me). She communicated with me in what I call the language of spirit.

At the time, I didn't know about Quan Yin. Today, with more knowledge, I realize it was Quan Yin, the Goddess and Divine Mother of Buddhism. Quan Yin is one of the most universally beloved of deities in the Buddhist Faith. It makes sense that I wouldn't see her legs because that's the way she is depicted universally, sitting low. I didn't see her legs yet she told me about my mother's leg. Buddhism is also the leading religion of the area I was going to visit. As the kids today would say, duh!!!!

I awoke the next morning and again I couldn't make sense of the dream or the message brought to me by the beautiful Chinese Lady. I began to wonder if something was going to happen to me during my upcoming trip. I decided to put it aside and wait for the pieces to fall into place. In any event, I decided not to-do anything about canceling the trip because she had said the leg would be all right.

About one month before l was due to go, my mother fell ill again and I figured I was going to have to cancel the trip. I kept postponing the cancellation hoping that her condition would improve. My mother had cancer and diabetes. She went to see a doctor for her cancer and, when she was going to get on the bus she smacked her shin against the step of the bus. The leg became extremely swollen and the sore became infected. She was told to keep off of her feet, or she could lose the leg. There was no way I was going to go on a trip and leave her that way, but I waited. The dream flashed before me often in those days, almost like an encouragement not to give up. About a week prior to my departure the leg started to heal. It was almost miraculous. She was completely healed by the time I was due to leave. It occurred to me that my faith was being tested.

The trip proved very spiritual for me! I visited holy shrines in Formosa, Hong Kong, Korea, Thailand, Nepal and India. It felt right! Coincidentally, there was another single woman traveling with the group whose birthday was the exact same day as mine. When we returned from an all-day trip to the communist Chinese border with Nepal, the tour director had arranged for a birthday cake and everyone in the hotel dining room celebrated with us. It was not only quite a surprise, but it also marked it as a special journey.

However, as in all things, there was good and evil evident. While my journey was spiritually positive, the negative side was also presented to me in Thailand. A man did astrology readings at our Bangkok hotel. I had a short reading and the man was very good in doing character analysis, which was the object of the short reading. He told me that he could do a longer, more detailed chart but that it would cost more money and would take more time. My curiosity about all things psychic and how people from different parts of the world use these gifts led me to ask him for a longer, more detailed chart. I agreed and paid him in advance, but never received the chart he promised. He was there to bilk the tourists.

At first I was very angry, not because of the money involved; at that time the rate of exchange made the amount negligible, but because this man was demeaning something I considered important to a great many people. Later I recognized that he too was part of my life's lesson, to help me understand that anything in life can be used for good or evil. It all depends on the individual's integrity and strength of character. It made me reinforce my belief that I would use it for the good and to help other people.

I remember a particular incident after my return from that trip. I had come home from work and I was very tired. My nephew Mike was doing homework, we had dinner and right after I said that I was taking shower and going to sleep. I went into the bathroom and smelled smoke. I called Mike over and asked if he smelled any smoke; he said no. I couldn't take a shower because I felt uncomfortable with the odor. I went back into my bedroom. A short while later I returned to the bathroom and this time the odor seemed even stronger. I called Mike and said, Please tell me if you smell any smoke. Again, Mike said he did not. I asked him to go down to the doorman and tell him that I was smelling smoke and that it should be investigated. Mike did as I asked. He loved going downstairs to the lobby and talking with the doormen and this presented a grand opportunity. He returned and told me they would investigate. I went back into the bathroom, but no longer smelled the smoke. About an hour later one of the building's staff knocked on the door. He came to inform me that a woman on the second floor had fallen asleep with a cigarette and had started a fire. No one had noticed the odor or smoke. They noticed it only when they checked the second floor, after we notified them. They tried knocking on her door, but got no answer. The woman was unconscious. They broke down the door and got her out in time to save her life with CPR by the ambulance personnel.

I realized that I had not been allowed to go take the shower because I needed to sound a warning and prevent the fire from spreading and endangering other lives including Mike's and my own. I thanked God and my spiritual guides for allowing me to save that woman's life and for the continued protection they offered the rest of us in the building.

That moment also brought back vividly the other occasion when I had smelled smoke on board the ship I hadn't realized it at the time but another of my psychic centers had been opened my intuitive sense of smell.

ENTER JOHN EDWARD

My life seemed like a see-saw. My changes were back and forth and back again. These changes were all forced on me when it was time to ease up and re-group. My friend Shala was looking for a place in which to live and do her Past Life Regressions. She took over my apartment in New York. I was unemployed at the time and was doing temporary assignments.

Shala called me after that and said that she was going to be on vacation for three weeks and asked if I would like to substitute for her. I agreed and was introduced into the world of financial investment where I worked happily for three weeks.

A few months after Shala's return to work, she again called and asked if I would be willing to come back for another temporary assignment which would last for another three weeks. I agreed. The employees were a closely-knit group. I felt right at home there and enjoyed the atmosphere. On her return, Shala asked if I would be interested in replacing her on a permanent basis as she was going into the Past Life Regressions full time. I said yes, discussed it with her boss and went to work there full time in June of that year.

The longer I remained the more I realized that everyone had to have been associated at some point in a prior lifetime. The coincidences were just too many. I had not told anyone that I had spiritual faculties or that I did readings. Shala, however, had mentioned it in conversation to another woman who worked there, "Prin". Actually, her name was "Perinda" her family called her "Princess" but even that had been shortened to Prin. It seems that Prin was very much into the psychic world. She loved having readings done and Shala told her to talk to me. One day Prin came up to my floor and stopped to talk to me. She said she would like to have a reading. She asked me how much I charged and I told her. I had a strange feeling but said nothing.

A couple of weeks later, I saw Prin again and said to her, "Prin, I want to explain something to you; I attach a great deal of importance too the spiritual work I do. Most people will take it for granted if they don't have to work for what they want, so if they don't have to work for a reading they will take what I say for granted. I didn't know why I felt compelled to explain this to her. She looked at me smiled and said, *I never thought about it that way, you are- right. I run everywhere to get readings and probably do tend to take them for granted anyway. My family says I'm a psychic junky.* We became very good friends after that. Of course, I did a reading for her not because we were friends but because I wanted to reinforce what l had said, about helping others.

Shortly, thereafter, Prin came to me and was very upset. She had received word that her son John, had been diagnosed with a brain tumor and she asked me to read her. John was about 15 years old at the time. She explained the situation and I listened with ALL of my senses. I told her that I didn't feel there was anything wrong with him at all. At that precise moment, John called her and the call was transferred to my desk where she was. I heard a one-sided conversation in which she explained to John that he had nothing wrong with him and that Lydia had said so. He became very upset and asked if his mother would take the word of a psychic over that of a doctor. She said of course not, that he would undergo all of the testing required, BUT that she believed what I said. John underwent all of the tests and they showed he did not have a tumor.

Prin was so impressed with what I had told her and the results of the testing that she couldn't stop talking about it. She brought other members of her family to have readings at psychic fairs and even arranged a group reading at her home. That's when I met her son John for the first time. While reading him in his home, I predicted that he would become a world famous psychic. He scoffed, because he saw himself as a normal, fun loving young man and what I was saying made him a bit nervous. I had never been more certain of anything. I felt strongly and told him, that the main reason for my trip to his home was to meet him, give him the information I gave him and to set, or fine tune, his vibration towards the spiritual world. That has already happened. I am referring to John Edward, medium, lecturer, and "best selling" author of. the book "One Last Time" among others. He has gone on to host the television program, "Crossing Over" with John Edward and later embarked on another show "Cross Country".

At this point in his life John Edward is undertaking another project in which he will be *creating a universal learning center* on the web. This *world wide type of university* will be up and running as of June 12, 2009 and can be accessed at: *www.InfiniteQuest.com.* There will be *spiritual and esoteric classes available* taught by teachers in all areas of the paranormal.

To get back to my beginnings with John and his family, my friendship with Prin grew quite profound and lasted until her death. Just before she passed, she asked John to call me and asked that I come to see her. She said to me, "I can't go on anymore. I'm not letting anyone else visit, but I wanted to see you once more. I don't want anyone to see me in this condition." I felt terrible and tried to prepare her for what was coming by telling her to call on her guides to give her strength. I brought her a pink quartz crystal to hold onto. We said a tearful farewell.

A few days later, at the funeral parlor, her son John told me that just before she passed she was crying for one of her sisters to take her down from the ceiling. Her soul was already preparing its departure from the body and was just hanging by the silver cord that united her to the physical life. She continued to call for her sister's help. Then she exclaimed, *Daddy, 0 My God, It's Beautiful!* And she passed. Evidently her father had come to greet her and helped her make her transition. Life takes strange turns. My experience in encouraging others to fulfill their spiritual destinies started with my friendship with Prin. Shortly thereafter, John embarked on his spiritual journey. I realized that one of my missions was spotting people with this ability and encouraging them to develop. As time passed, others came into my path for the same encouragement and many have achieved great success.

After I did my initial reading for Prin, word got around the office "that I was psychic". One of the executives asked for and got a reading from me. When I was finished the executive said, "I'm impressed, you are very good." On another occasion, I remember that I got this strong impression that one of the women in the office would be pregnant. I jokingly said them, *Ladies you'd better be careful because someone here is going to be pregnant and I really don't know who it is.* They all made jokes and laughed but I didn't mind.

Not long after, a new receptionist was hired. Shortly after she started, she received a phone call and started to cry. She told the office manager that she had to resign, because there was a serious problem with her husband, and she had also just been informed that she was pregnant. The reason she was crying was not about the pregnancy, but the problem with her husband. One of the women came running over to me and said, *Look, she's the one with the pregnancy.* There were many, occasions like this.

I should also mention that I become particularly intuitive when it comes to family and to those people with whom I am very close. Anytime there was something out of the ordinary, I would dream about it and mention it to my boss. He would tell his wife and invariably we would discuss it when she either called, or came by the, office to tell, me it was so. They are very warm and caring people.

One such instance occurred when we moved to new offices. I had a dream that his wife had had a baby boy and that their middle daughter was complaining that her mother didn't pay attention to her any more. I mentioned this to him the next morning and he started to laugh. He said, *My wife is pregnant again and Helen (his middle daughter) told me those exact words last night.* The best part was when she delivered a beautiful baby boy, Gilly. All of these children that I mention are now grown into adulthood, but my memories of them continue.

Back at the office, another one of my friends, had been married a while and wanted to have a baby. During that time I went on a pilgrimage to Medjugorge, a Shrine in honor of the Virgin Mary in Yugoslavia. While there, I prayed that she would become pregnant. I wanted to see her happy. I lit a candle and brought back a medal from the Shrine for each of the girls in the office. Shortly thereafter she became pregnant.

She progressed very well and one day after lunch I looked at her and all I saw was what appeared to be a large pink balloon in place of her stomach. I didn't say anything, but a bit later she mentioned that she had gotten the results of her test and, before she could go further I blurted, *It's a girl.* Ann, my co-worker, looked at me and said " I just found out. How did you know?" I told her about the pink balloon in place of her stomach and she just stared at me. Then she continued and said, *The rest of the story is that it's twins.* we were all ecstatic.

DREAMS

As you have learned by now, my whole life has been impacted, enhanced and guided by dreams.

A card I received recently defined dreams as follows: dreams: n. plural - a series of images, sometimes pleasant and tantalizing, that appear in the mind of a person during sleep.

The problem with this description is that It doesn't include the *nightmare* dreams, the *prophetic* dreams, etc.

Why are dreams so important? It has been said that dreams are a portal into the soul. In them we play out our dramas and desires and confront our fears. Sometimes the soul simply flies off to a place where it can communicate with beings vibrating at a much higher and faster level of energy than our own. Dreams are a state of being in which our souls can express their true natures and be free to explore, communicate and relate to souls on higher planes of existence.

Therefore, it is necessary to train our subconscious mind to send and receive messages as symbols in such a way that the meaning is clear to us upon awakening.

To those who have chosen to develop spiritually, dreams can be very clear. The symbols and events often appear in full and colorful detail. Their meanings, however, are understood more easily as we and time progress.

Sometimes, when the dream is predictive in nature, its full meaning will not be understood by the dreamer until the event happens. Only then does it become crystal clear; as when I dreamed about the beautiful Chinese lady who told me about "the leg that would heal." My mother had not injured herself yet. When she did I kept moving ahead with plans for my trip to the Orient. I did not doubt the dream, even though I had no point of reference to help me put it into perspective. When the injury did occur, my mind flashed back to the dream and I understood. The process requires strong faith, a belief in a source higher than ourselves or guardian angels that either volunteer or are appointed to help us.

I will give you a few current *dream occurrences* in my life and show why there are forewarnings that things make no sense at the time of the dream:

911 and the World Trade Center bombing:

About one month before 911, I had a dream that I was in a building that housed my real estate office in Plantation, Florida. All of a sudden everything was moving and shaking and, in the dream, I thought it was an earthquake. I started running for all I was worth to get out. Outside there were rocks flying and the air was full of smoke and flying debris. I kept running and running, crossed a street and tried to take shelter next to a building that was not being affected and watched as my own office building tumbled down.

I woke up shaking and wondered if I was being shown something that was going to happen to me and/or my office. It took me a while to calm down and when I did, I called my friend Judy and told her about it. Since nothing happened, I just let it slide and never gave it more thought.

As an aside, and so that you are clear about timing and symbolism in dreams I should tell you that TWO YEARS PRIOR, when I lived in New Jersey, I worked for Dow Jones Television as an assistant to the President of the station. WBIS+TV and the offices from where the news was broadcast, was located in the World Financial Center.. It was directly connected by an overhead, enclosed walkway, to the World Trade Center. After the explosion, you may have seen the walkway still hanging from the side of the WTC building that it had been connected to. That walkway and the trains that ran underneath were part of my trip to and from work every day.

As it happens, prior to 911, the TV station was sold and I eventually returned to Florida. Otherwise, I might have been caught up in the horror as well. Ironically, my subconscious emotional connection to the area had not been cut, and somehow I chose the 911 week to travel to the New York/New Jersey area to do readings. I had dinner in New York City with a friend the night before and witnessed via TV from my hotel room the horror of the attacks on the buildings. It was then I realized what my dream the prior month had meant. While the attacks were going on, my friend, Judy, from Plantation, Florida called me at the hotel and all she could say was "your dream, your dream that's what it meant"!

I witnessed the event as in the dream. I watched it from a building that was safe, and where I could later see the survivors from Morgan Stanley, being transported by buses, cars and limousines to another of the company's buildings. These offices were located right next door to the hotel where I was staying in New Jersey.

The Link to Childhood Friends

Maurice (Moose) Clement —
On Sunday night December 4th into Monday December 5th - around 4AM – - I had a dream that I was walking with a man who was tall, husky, balding and he wore a brown leather, bomber-type jacket. I knew him in the dream but couldn't identify him when I woke up. We were talking amiably, like old friends, and when we reached a certain destination, I turned around to see something behind me. When I turned back around, my friend, had walked a little ahead and fallen down. I was about to run over to him when I saw this magnificent Angel all encompassed in white light approach my friend, surround him in white light and whisk him straight up into the light and heaven. In the dream I just stood there looking up at the incredible sight.

I immediately woke up. My first thought was oh, oh, who's passing around me? I was sad, upset and couldn't go back to sleep so I got out of bed, had coffee and puttered around the house.

On Tuesday December 6th, I received a Christmas card from my friend Ann Piazza. In it she mentioned that Moose, a nickname for a childhood friend and Bill Leavy, another childhood friend, had asked about me. When I received the card I thought, how nice of them to remember me.

The following day, Wednesday, December 7th, I received an e-mail from Ann, telling me that Moose had died early morning on Monday, December

5th. The e-mail said that he died in his sleep. I called Ann and I went through this whole explanation of the dream I'd had and asked what Moose had looked like as an adult, as I hadn't seen him since I was about 17-18 years old. She described him as "Heavy-set, not fat, and balding just like I'd seen in the dream. I told her that in my dream he had fallen down . She answered, no, that his wife had told her when she was at the funeral parlor that he had passed of a heart attack in his sleep.   I was very determined to get my point across that he had fallen down , but Ann was just as determined to quote what she had heard; that he died in his sleep from a heart attack. I asked her to call his wife and just mention what I said about the Angel and his going straight up to heaven.

That same evening, Ann called back and I could tell she was shaken up. I asked what was wrong. She explained that she had called Dotty, Moose's wife, and told her about my dream and mentioned that I thought he had fallen down. Dotty explained that he HAD fallen down. They were in bed and Moose was due to get up for work very early that morning. She heard him fall out of the bed and she went to him to try to help him but he was a big man and she couldn't. He died in the process. That confirmed to Ann that indeed Moose had fallen by the side of the bed and that I, in turn, had seen him at the time he was passing.

When Ann had this conversation with Dotty, she was very annoyed that I had given that information because she didn't believe in psychics or any of that stuff. It seems, however, that Moose DID believe in all things psychic and probably knew that I was an easy way for him to communicate that he was ok. He showed himself to me as a much younger person so that his wife and, eventually, I would recognize him. The brown jacket was one that he wore to go to work .

Some time later, Ann called me again to let me know that his wife, Dotty, had called her again and that she was sorry that she had gotten annoyed, but at the time, she was:

  1) mad that he had left her,

  2) mad that there wasn't anything she could do about it and that

  3) the communication had come through a psychic, me.

Dotty told Ann that once she started to calm down and started to reason things out, she was grateful for the verification and asked Ann to let me know how grateful she was to know that he was ok.

Salvatore Alicata—
I have a childhood best friend, Rita Wright-Lucchesi, with whom I have kept in touch throughout the years. There were times we didn't see one another for years, but we'd always find a way to talk or get in touch with one another. Rita's sister, Fran, married Salvatore (Sal). We were all from the same group of friends and always through one person or another we would hear about the others.

Sal, had been ill for a very long time. Sometime during the first or second Sunday in October of 2008 I was sitting in church and was meditating and participating in the service. I opened my eyes and looked up and I had a vision of Sal, at a much younger age, standing in mid-air looking down at me and smiling. I said to myself this can't be and closed my eyes again. A few minutes later I opened them, looked up and there was Sal still standing in mid-air. When I finally acknowledged him mentally, the vision disappeared.

When I reached home I immediately called my friend Rita and asked if Sal had passed. She said no. I explained what had happened to me in church and I told her that it wouldn't be too much longer. She started to think out loud and said to me you know Fran told me he's been talking about seeing his kids and others from the past. It must have been during the review of his life, in a subconscious state, and when he spoke about the people from the past, that maybe he saw you and you, in turn, saw him while at church.

Late on the night of 25th of November, 2008, I was sitting watching TV and I heard this awful noise coming from the outside. It scared me and I couldn't place what direction it was coming from or whether it was human or animal. It was loud, scary and very disconcerting. I called my next door neighbor to see if she heard anything and she said No. I asked her to go towards the front of her house and listen. She kept her mobile telephone with her as she went, got a flashlight and went out. All I could hear was: *"O My God, O My God, I can't believe it. It's huge. It's bigger than your dog or mine."* I finally asked her, is it an owl? I thought it might have sounded like an owl at one point and she said *"yes, it's an owl but I've never seen anything so huge."* I got spooked!

The next morning I received an e-mail that Sal had passed the night before at the same time as I heard the noise from the owl. I returned the e-mail to my friend Rita and wrote out all that had happened the night before at the time that Sal had passed. She wrote back saying: VERY Spooky, but I'll tell Fran what you said. It seems she took my e-mails with her and let Fran and their children read them after the memorial service for Sal.

I sent a Mass Card for Sal to Fran. She responded with a note: *I want to thank you for the mass card, but most of all for the help that you gave me with the 'receiving' of Sal. It was a great comfort to me and the children to know that he is all right.*
Love, Fran

This is part of a group of friends who forged a link in life that transcends time.

For those who choose not to develop this ability, dreams continue in symbol form and messages are not always understood clearly. Some people insist that they do not dream and have never dreamed. They may not remember their dreams, but the fact is that everyone dreams and that dreams can have a therapeutic effect. Medical and clinical psychologists and researchers have identified the various stages and cycles of sleep and have amassed considerable evidence that the *rapid eye* movement or *REM* phase indicates that the person is dreaming.

I believe that people who can't remember them are subconsciously afraid of dreaming or encountering things that their conscious minds cannot face. As I have recounted earlier, and speaking from personal experience, I blocked my dream memory as a child. I might say that during that period my spiritual messengers were getting a busy signal.

Only the overwhelming need to help my mother enabled me to overcome my fears and remove the defensive barriers I had constructed. Perhaps presenting me with that necessity in crisis, is the way my spiritual guides chose to get through to me.

This incident also demonstrates the power of love. I believe that love is one of the great forces that can help us to overcome almost anything. We should practice more love of one another and not harbor thoughts that can stop us from progressing to a better, happier life. Bear in mind that thought is action! What we think or visualize is what we create and what we create we project into our every day lives. Whether that power is used for good or evil, positive or negative, is up to each individual.

NEGATIVE DREAMS/
THE SEARCH FOR ANSWERS

I am not what is commonly referred to as a Christian fundamentalist, one who takes every word of the Bible literally. I have been exposed to too many cultures and religions for that. I am, however, a Christian and I do believe strongly in the scriptural promise: Seek and ye shall find.

To approach this subject, I am regressing to a point in my life just prior to my move to Miami . Although still working and immersed in the field of spirit, I had a feeling that change was upon me again. I decided to seek" and I did find. The end of the year took me on a trip to Puerto Rico where I celebrated the New Year. While on that trip I met my second husband. As life would have it, a number of years later I re-married. Unfortunately, this time I didn't listen to my own dreams. Before the wedding, I had the same recurring nightmare for three days and kept trying to rationalize it as fear of going into another marriage or making a mistake. I never believed that my guardian angels would let me fail. YES, ladies and gentlemen, unfortunately for me, they tried and I didn't listen, or couldn't be objective for myself this time.

He was an established attorney and I was working for the financial investment firm in New York. Moving to Florida was the compromise. In 1990 we relocated to Miami, married and went on with life. I got a job as an assistant to the head of a Venezuelan Bank in Miami. A year later, I understood my nightmares as they came to a head and by 1991, we divorced.

I kept wondering what I was supposed to learn out of the situation and concluded three things:

- a) I learned that when emotions get in the way, clarity does not come until one is re-balanced.

- b) I needed to be independent again in order to do that.

- c) I needed to be in Miami for what followed.

Had I not married and heeded my guide's intervention, my transition to Miami might have been different, or not at all.

LYDIA'S PERSONAL VALIDATION FROM SPIRIT

I remained in Florida, working and looking around to interest myself in something else. I decided that I would look into the real estate field. It turned out to be a total re-training but I found it interesting and did well. After the required number of years, I got my Broker's License and opened my own firm. During this time period, while I was not entirely absent from the psychic field, I wasn't as involved. I took a break to get re-balanced and get myself back into spirit mode. My work in real estate dealing with people again brought me back.

While I had set the standard of waiting until it was time for me to go back to work with spirit, spirit didn't want to wait any longer and came after me in the form of my friends William and Maria Perez.

WHERE DOES THE UNKNOWN TAKE US? Far, believe me. At the end of August, 1993 my friends Maria and William came back from a trip to Spain. On their return William brought back a thesis by a Spanish doctor and asked if I would be interested in translating it into English. The topic was breast cancer, the various procedures and treatments, historical research data, etc.

Because of its technical material, it took me through the end of December to complete. After I finished the assignment and it was submitted to the doctor in Spain, I saw an ad by South Miami Hospital about a free Breast Cancer Symposium being jointly sponsored by the hospital and the Don

Shula Foundation. My translation job had roused my interest, so I decided to attend.

The symposium was hosted by Michele Gillen, then anchor of Channel 4 WTVJ-NBC, and I was extremely impressed with the professional presentation and the quality of the participants. I even asked questions during the question and answer period that followed. At the conclusion of the symposium, cards for a free mammogram were distributed to some of the attendees. I was one of those who received a card. I scheduled an appointment for a mammogram and was found to have a lump in my left breast. Needless to say I was shocked; I had no idea.

The lump could not be felt during a regular examination and I had experienced no pain or discomfort. I had had the mammogram done only because the Spanish doctor's thesis had aroused my interest in the subject, which in turn led me to attend the symposium where I was given the card. Some might say that was a strange sequence of events. I know it was anything but strange.

I was told that I had to schedule another, more precise mammogram, and the lump showed up again. This was followed by a sonogram to rule out the possibility of a cyst. It was not. The final diagnosis was that I had a very small tumor.

1) It was recommended that I see a surgeon. He turned out to be one of the doctors on the symposium panel to whom I, PERSONALLY, had directed a question to from the audience.

2) I was uncertain as to which treatment to follow. It took me a while to arrive at a decision, but I did eventually, again, *by coincidence.* I was meeting with an attorney about a legal matter. I asked him to deal with it as quickly as possible because I had a medical problem that I needed to take care of before the end of the year. He asked me what was wrong and I told him. He then proceeded to tell me his story.

He had been diagnosed as having melanoma, the most deadly form of skin cancer, and was given six months to live. He researched the major medical facilities and doctors in New York, Boston, Cleveland, and Baltimore and found that the best doctor was right in South Miami Hospital. He had the surgery done by him. I asked for the doctor's name and it turned out to be the same doctor to which I had been referred and the one to whom I had addressed my questions at the symposium. My doubts were resolved, my course clear.

    3) The very next day, I called the doctor and made an appointment. He looked over the x-rays, verified what I had been told before and said that I could go one of two ways:

        a) Wait to see if the lump developed any significant change; or

        b) Go ahead and get it removed. I told him I would think about it.

It took me as long as it took to walk from the examining room to the receptionist's desk. What more did I need? Instinctively I knew he was the right man to do whatever was necessary and that there was no point in postponing my decision any longer.

I asked the receptionist how long it would take to schedule the surgery and she said that it usually, took a while, and maybe longer because it was so close to the holidays. I asked her to check and she called. She looked at me and said *how unusual they have an opening on Monday morning.* She then checked to see if the doctor who would do the needle biopsy was available, and again she said, *yes - -* more coincidences? I had gotten my validation and without expecting it. I asked her to book me.

The following Monday morning I went into South Miami Hospital and had the procedure done. The small tumor was removed and, thankfully, It was benign. What would have happened if I had not translated that Thesis or gone to that seminar? I still think about it!

I believe that everything has a purpose or a meaning, so I can't believe in random coincidence. That is why I remain impressed by the sequence of events. First the translation; then the free lecture; the free mammogram; the talk with the lawyer who gave me the confidence to go see the doctor that had been referred; then the doctor himself and being able to schedule so quickly and so close to a holiday weekend. I think even the most ardent believer in coincidence would have to wonder about the possibility of a guiding hand (or hands) behind this string of coincidences. I was very grateful to God and wondered how I could ever thank him enough for yet another miracle.

Therefore, if something is brought to your attention (whether it's a personal validation, warning, or new direction) follow through. It can possibly eliminate a painful situation, a sorrow or save your life, follow through!

Recuperation Time and Interesting Events:

While recuperating from my surgery I visited with a friend in Miami, who is also psychic. When she finished my reading and we were having a general conversation, she told me a story of a young woman who had gone to her for a reading. The young woman was supposed to have gotten married. One day, her fiancée went to work and at the end of the day, clocked out with the guard at the gate and was never heard from again. The young woman was beside herself. My friend asked me if I could pick up anything. My only comment was: I see him on the ground surrounded by jungle and there are three men around him. Unfortunately, I couldn't pick up anything else. I said my goodbyes and went home.

After I had recuperated enough to travel, I made arrangements to go on a *thank you for all I have pilgrimage* which took me to a number of religious shrines in Venezuela. I returned fully emotionally and spiritually restored to Miami..

A few months after my return from the pilgrimage, I again visited my friend to let her know how my trip to Venezuela had gone. Before I left her home that day, something prompted me to ask her about the woman whose fiancée had gone missing. She answered that she had not heard anything else and that as far as she knew he was still missing. A few days later she called me and was very excited. She said, "You're not going to believe what I am going to tell you. Later on the day when you visited me and asked me about the young woman's fiancée, I got a call from her to tell me that the police found him dead in the everglades which is the jungle area you saw.

They were able to identify him only because of his dental records and the clothes he was wearing on the day he went missing. As my friend spoke, I got the same vision of three men surrounding the missing man and, again, in the jungle area. I mentioned this to her and she said, *You are probably right, because he was a very big man it would have taken at least three to overpower him.* I have not heard anything since and probably never will

As I write this story, I still don't know why I was given the information to begin with, or what brought about my response of seeing him in the jungle.

At the time my only thought was feeling sorry for the lady whose fiancée was missing and gave out the information I received.

I always try to follow the rule I learned when I first started my training, *when you see something, do not hold back the information. Even if it doesn't make sense to you it doesn't necessarily mean it won't to someone else.* The only thing I can think of is that my training kicked in at that time and I just let it out!

LYDIA'S TESTIMONIALS/ CLIENT VALIDATIONS

In writing this book, it was suggested that I include validation or testimonials of my work over the years. I found it ironic to have to supply them, as those who have been read by me, know that I don't remember what I say during a reading once it is over. In order to comply, however, I have asked some clients that I have read over the years, to write the testimonials for me and they follow:

From HB (Computer Consultant)

I find comfort in our readings; when I am worried about something and you tell me that it will be all right, I know by now that it will be.

Skeptics have told me that in order for a reading to be considered accurate, events should come to fruition within the near future. It has been my experience that you are not shown events that will occur within a specific time-frame and-that they can occur within weeks, months or even years:

Example: While I was working as a computer consultant, you told me that a Director of Data Processing for whom I had previously worked would ask me to do another project, but at a different company than before. Over a year later a man for whom I had worked in the Home Office of a smaller retail chain called to ask me to do a project for him at his new place of business - - a much larger retail chain.

It has been my experience that negative predictions can be used to avoid negative events.

Example:The first time she warned me that my son would become a young, "unwed father," I cautioned him to be careful, which he didn't take too seriously. She gave me the same warning in the next reading and again I passed it on to him. During my last reading, she didn't mention it, so when it was time for me to ask my questions, I asked whether she still saw the baby. She did not. I believe that the warnings I passed on to my son impressed upon him that this was a serious matter and that he needed to be careful.

She warned me that my son would get into drug-related trouble. A few months later, he was stopped for speeding, with a "roach-clip" sitting in plain view on the back seat. He and his friend were arrested for marijuana possession.

More Examples:As my father's health declined, his third wife became disenchanted with their marriage. Lydia told me that she was enraged about the turn her life had taken and that when she finally exploded, her rage would be directed toward me. Within weeks she had a tantrum and for a year disallowed me from calling their home or visiting.

She threatened to put my father into a nursing home, which Lydia said she would do, and she did. Lydia told me at the next reading that she would be asking for more than the $600 per month we had arranged for her to get from Dad's brokerage account to pay the difference between the nursing home bill and Dad's long term care payment, plus his social security check. She had been receiving precisely $600 per month and she then started asking for money for miscellaneous items. Lydia warned me not to allow her to obtain "signing power" for him, and I responded that I didn't think she would attempt it. Within a few weeks, she announced that she wanted sole Power of Attorney, which we successfully blocked.

When my son was young, he had unusual experiences, which frightened him terribly. In particular, a dark-haired petite woman was appearing to him in his room in the middle of the night. He would hide under his covers until he eventually fell asleep. Lydia advised me that she was his psychic guide and didn't intend to frighten him; since she was "around" him he could simply say aloud at anytime that she was frightening him and that he didn't want her to return. He did and much to his relief, she stopped coming. Lydia said that his abilities came from his father's side of the family; my mother-in-law confirmed occurrences in her family.

Plants were shaking in two of our houses, as if someone had taken hold of each and shaken it. Only I had experienced this. Lydia advised that our dead were communicating that they were with us in a way we could understand. Lydia said that in particular, my recently departed father-in-law was "visiting" periodically (as he did with his other children) and Lydia also identified a particular chair (in the family room) he sat in when with us. My husband didn't believe me when I said the plants were shaking nor that his father visited us. One day when he was alone in the house, a plant located close to his "father's chair" began to shake.

J & K
(Transportation & Real Estate Development)

My Wife and I had gone to see John Edward several times and we asked him to recommend someone for a psychic reading. Without hesitation he recommended Lydia Clar. Our first visit was in 1998. Since then so many events that Lydia described, (which at the time made no sense to me or my wife) came to pass over the years. Lydia is a remarkable psychic and has a warm caring sense about her. You can feel her presence in a room and I find it enlightening and very spiritual. Let me share some of the remarkable readings that I've had over the years with her.

In one session Lydia told me that I would be selling my business. She saw me, my father and brothers all signing legal papers. At the time I never would have believed any one would ever buy our company or that our family would ever agree to sell our business. My family owned a transportation business, which was founded by my father. We all worked together for 24 years. Lydia was telling me we were going to sell. She described the trials and tribulations I would have with my brothers. She gave detailed descriptions of the men and women who were interested in buying the company. She also told me about buyers that were just looking, as well as those that were really interested. For whatever reason, every time there was a new buyer, the sale would not happen. Then after 3 years she described a company that was interested in buying us out and said that the sale to this particular company would definitely happen by the end of the year. At the end of the year we entered into an agreement with that company and by the following March, the company was sold to the investment banking company that she had described

In another session, she warned me that my father was sick. Although I was not aware of it at the time, he was currently being treated by doctors. She told me that his current treatment was incorrect and that he should immediately see another doctor for additional testing. She also said that if he didn't, the problem in his throat would get worse and the problem could possibly be irreversible. I told my father and he said I was crazy. He said that he was currently being treated for allergies, and that he was sure that's all it was. He also said he would not go to another doctor. His doctor told him the discomfort he was feeling in his throat was due to a nasal drip brought on by allergies and he would need to give the medicine some time before he would feel relief. Knowing my father wouldn't listen to me and that the information I received was coming from Lydia, I panicked. I knew I needed to go to a higher authority so I told my Mother. That week she immediately made him go to another doctor for a second opinion. The new doctor took ex-ray's and found a tumor in his throat that was causing allergy-like symptoms. The doctors told him if the tumor was not removed immediately it could continue to grow and lead to more serious complications. He had it removed and has been fine ever since.

While I was working at the transportation company, Lydia continued to say "after you sell your company I see you in a new business, something to do with real estate." She said it would be very successful and saw my wife-traveling south with me. After the sale of the company was concluded, my wife and I went to Florida and bought a house. During that time, I ran into a man who had lived in my hometown in N.J. He had also just moved to Florida and was beginning to look along the intercoastal for properties that could be developed. He asked me if I was interested in joining him. I remember thinking "AHHHH this is was Lydia was talking about" so I said "YES". We formed a partnership and began purchasing properties in Florida. We now own several large development sights and our properties' values have more than doubled over the last 2 years.

Prior to the sale of the family business, I owned a small 12-unit property with a friend Louis Morilla in New Jersey. We spent approximately two years bringing it up to code and generally refurbishing and fixing it. When it was finally complete we rented out all of the units and we thought we would have this forever. At that point in time, I went to another session with Lydia. She said I would sell it and double my money. When I told this to my partner he said, "why would we sell it? We just did all this work and no one would pay us double in only 2 years." A few weeks later he received an offer for the purchase of the property at double the amount we paid for the building. We happily sold it.

Prior to my marriage to my current wife "K", we were living in a beautiful home which I had received as part of a divorce settlement. In another reading with Lydia, she told me that she saw that (unbeknownst to me) "K" was not happy living there and that she saw us moving. This was a home I built myself and which I thought I would have forever. I told Lydia she was definitely wrong on this one. She gave the same information to "K" during a reading she had. To "K", however, she also described the home we would buy. She went into the detail of the difficulties we would have during and after the purchase. Lydia saw "K's" father (deceased) standing in water pointing to Bricks and shaking his head. This time, none of us new what the heck she was seeing or what it meant. Why would her father be standing in water pointing to a Brick foundation? A year and a half later, we went through a long drawn out closing on a house that was exactly as Lydia had described. We finally closed in December, '04, while there was still snow on the ground. When the snow melted, we noticed that the brick foundation in our pool house was under water. The building had been built at the wrong grade level and consequently, all the run-off water (from the snow) was running from the main house like a stream into the brick foundation and then through it into the pool house. I wasn't surprised in the least. Fortunately because of Lydia's insight, I negotiated, at closing, an escrow to be held for one year. Lydia's reading had saved us $50,000 worth of damage that we would have had to pay if we hadn't taken her reading seriously. Although when we initially receive information it sometimes doesn't make sense, we are now convinced that at some point it will. It always has.

DJ (Psychic Medium
& Author of: *Angels Whisper to us~
Decoding the Messages in Daydreams)*

Finding Lydia:The day I found Lydia Clar was a magical moment. I was reading John Edward's book, "One Last Time" and read how Lydia had influenced his life. I had been in one of those "hell on earth" periods and was desperately in need of guidance. Lydia's address was listed as Central Avenue in Jersey City. My family had owned a flower shop, St. Jude's, on Central Avenue, so the feeling of serendipity was unmistakable. I called her number. She answered the phone and said, "I never answer this phone my assistant does. I haven't had a cancellation in three months, and I have one this morning. How fast can you be here?" Two hours later I was sitting in front of her and the first thing she said to me was, "You have a gift and you are not using it!" That was the beginning of a relationship that I have come to value beyond words. Lydia is my friend, but above all, my mentor and guide. It is her well-balanced spirituality, psychic ability and incredible sense of humor that has enabled me to release fear and embrace my role as a psychic messenger. She has kept me on track, even coming to me in dreams. She helped give me the confidence I needed to deliver a message from the Archangels that resulted in my writing a book: Angels Whisper to us~ Decoding the Messages in Daydreams.

For this I am forever grateful.

The Power of Prayer: Lydia reinforced how important it is to have faith, and the power of prayer, no matter what your religious background. Once I went to see her, and as soon as I sat down, she asked me "Do you pray to the Infant of Prague?" I replied that yes, I had been praying to him but felt that my prayers had been answered, so I stopped. "Well he wants you to keep praying, so you had better start again!" she replied in that wonderful no-nonsense way she has about her. Ok then, you better believe I started praying again.

Ghosts: There was a very old house in the town where I used to own a business. I was constantly drawn to this house and didn't know why. I started dreaming of a woman with red hair. She was sitting on the steps of the house and talking to me about the people who had lived there. I started to feel she had been murdered there. The dreams were getting more and more vivid, until one night she started to materialize in front of me. Nothing like that had ever happened to me before. My mother was always seeing dead people, but I spent most of my time hiding under the blankets, praying they wouldn't show themselves to me. I screamed for her to go to God, to the light, as per Lydia's instructions, and thought "Lydia where are you when I need you." By then she had moved to Florida. I had been afraid to go to sleep, pacing the floors until I was too exhausted to stay awake.

Soon after, I found out that Lydia was coming to New Jersey and I would be able to see her in person in just a few days. After our greeting, Lydia asked me to give her something to hold. I had on a silver bracelet with the image of a woman's face. Lydia took it, closed her eyes and began to meditate. When she spoke she said: "I am seeing a woman with red hair and a diadem on her head." She came through immediately. Lydia told me that by praying for her, and telling her to go to God, she was able to leave the house that she felt bound to, and would guide me through this next part of my life. When we were through, she gave me the bracelet back and we were admiring it under the light. I had never noticed before, but the small face had wavy hair and a diadem on her head! Thank you, Lydia

Lydia to the rescue!For a year I had been struggling with getting a divorce, closing my store and trying to find a new place to live. The divorce was final, the store was closed, but after months of looking I still had not found a new home. I had been following the "signs" I was receiving from the other side and praying, but nothing seemed to be right. I was working with a realtor whom I trusted and really liked. When I found out that her dog and cat had the same name as my dog and cat, Angel and Shadow, I knew I was on the right track.

One Sunday, I had been driving around in circles, not able to find the street I was looking for. I was hot, tired and on the verge of tears. I pulled out my cell phone and dialed Lydia. "Please, Lydia, talk to your guides, talk to my guides, talk to your angels, but please help me, because I can't do this anymore!"

Lydia took a breath and in her best 'calm down and pull yourself together' voice she told me to get today's paper. She said that I was looking in one area, but I would see something in another area. It would be bold and stand out.

I drove home and got out the paper. I had been searching for homes in a few towns just north of where I lived, but I guess God had other plans. Sure enough, just as Lydia predicted, there was an ad for a house in the town I was living in, but in a different section, one that was very charming. It caught my eye because of the bold, black lines around it. It was right across the street from the river and just a few blocks away from my family. It came on the market on May 24th, my birthday. I called Lydia and she described the house before I even told her what it looked like. A few months later the house became mine, and I couldn't be happier.

I.C. (Banking)

My first reading with Lydia Clar occurred around May of 1999. Her first words to me during that reading were the description of an older man, lounging back in a chair, with gray hair in a crew cut. "Does that mean anything to you? She asked and I replied yes. Several moments later, Lydia asked if the name Harold meant anything to me. My grandfather's name was Harold and he had gray hair which he wore in a crew cut.

Back in December of, I believe, 2000, I had a reading with Lydia and during that reading she spoke of an up-coming problem with a mortgage. At the time, my parents were buying a condo in Westchester, NY and that was the only mortgage that I could think of where there could be issues. Lydia advised me that whoever name is on the mortgage should come off as soon as possible or a name should not go on a mortgage because problems will arise that will take time and a lot of effort to correct. She was very insistent of this potential problem but that it would be resolved.

Three months passed and I decided to get a home equity loan to do remodeling on my house. I called a bank, gave them the information that was needed and the woman on the other end of the phone informed me that everything I had told her was correct, except there was a mortgage on my credit report that had a bankruptcy attached to it. As a result of divorce, I had given my old house to my ex-husband and he had not refinanced or taken my name off the property and the mortgage. This was the start of a 7 month nightmare of trying to get my name off the mortgage which then went into default. Endless attorney's, state representative, to senators offices could not provide any help. The end result was that after many months and a lot of effort, I had my name removed from the mortgage and taken off the deed.

In March of 2003 I had another reading with Lydia Clar. The environment that I was working in had been rather unpleasant at times. Even through unpleasant times at work, I was close to my boss and knew a lot about his life, both at work and away from work. During that March, 2003, Lydia spoke of a man that I worked with and described his life in great detail from marriage problems to issues with his children to a struggle taking place in his life at that time. I could confirm all of this information due to my relationship with him. The gentleman that I worked with would be leaving the company soon Lydia advised, and after his departure the environment at work would improve. Two days after the reading, he resigned and took another job. Within days of his leaving, life at work dramatically changed. The tension at work had lifted and my work environment began to improve.

In 1999 I suffered three losses in a period of six months: my mother, my first husband, and my canine companion of seventeen years, my Irish Wolfhound, Larry. That third loss over whelmed me so much that I decided I needed confirmation that we do survive the change called death. I set out to book a private reading with someone I could trust. At that time I was reading John Edward's book "One Last Time". In that story there was a reference to Lydia Clar and the events of a reading where she outlined Edward's current life and his future; his journey to come, working as a medium before large audiences.

My initial reading and the several more that followed with this remarkable psychic all had a common thread: a visitor from spirit who made herself known to me through Lydia. The little girl indicated that I was her mother, but I was childless in this lifetime. I argued with Lydia that there must be some mistake. Thankfully and because of her lifetime of experience and true confidence in her work with spirit, Lydia stood by her messages; the child was my daughter.

I was not to uncover further evidence of this child's existence for a couple of years. Then in 2002 I received many more validations from spirit through other mediums that corroborated Lydia's first message. Each time the inner beauty and great love of this child in Spirit came to embrace me. Finally through extensive research and validation through original documents of the 13th century and contemporary chroniclers of the times, I determined that this spirit entity was indeed my daughter; a little girl who drowned in 1294 in a moat of her mother's estate at Woodham Ferrers Hall in Essex, England; a child I came to know as Martha Douglas.

Because Lydia had a reputation for impeccable honesty in her readings, not to mention a rather strong stubborn streak when she knew she was right, I allowed myself to accept her message about my daughter in spirit. Since that time I have received so much love and wonderful communication from Martha to which I credit Lydia Clar. Her work opened the door for me to a new world of spirit communication. Many other well know and well tested mediums since have validated Lydia's messages for me. But it was her initial words that will forever be etched in my mind. The reading had such an impact on my life that I have now written and published three books written with spirit. I will never forget her first message: 'Now listen to me; this little girl says she is your daughter,' and from those few words I have been led to a great miracle in my life.

NMcC (Human Resources)

In February, 2004 Lydia told me there were going to be upsets for me at work. She said she felt my supervisor was in trouble and that he would be leaving the company by the end of May. I was also told I would be presented with an option for my departure about two months later and that I should be careful because Lydia felt my employer was going to try to give me less than I was entitled to. She also told me to stick to my guns if this happened because I would get what I wanted.

Well, the pressure was put on my supervisor and he resigned from the company at the end of May. Then came the end of July (two months later) and, as predicted, I was presented with two different options regarding my departure, both of which would have given me less than I was entitled to! This lead me to take legal action, which delayed my actual departure date but Lydia was right on target. I was presented with options two months after my supervisor left and they were both less than I was entitled to.

I consulted Lydia two other times on this matter during the next 9 months and was told I was on the right track and to stick to my guns because the company would settle. She even gave me the time frame she felt I could expect a conclusion to this matter. So I followed her advice and sure enough the company settled around the date given! Not only that, the settlement was more than I had anticipated!

SS (Retired Police Department)

In 1998 I lost my mother, Mary, to a disease called interstitial lung disease. It was a life-altering loss for me as we were very close. My mother never smoked but lost her life to a disease that slowly takes your lung volume away.

For years she worked as a tea packer at Lipton Tea and Standard Brands where she and others packed tea, coffee, jello powder, ice tea powder and the like. It seems after years of exposure, the dust from those items caused the disease. I honestly believe that you never get over the loss itself, but with time and good friends it starts to heal.

My mother and I have always been spiritual and believe in heaven and reincarnation. The only solace that still brings me peace is that someday, when I'm gone we will always be together again. I remember my mother saying to me towards the end "if anyone can find a way to connect with one another for us to talk it's you."

In 2001 I heard from my friend Susan, that she and her husband had been seeing a medium named Lydia Clar and that because I was so depressed they thought it might help for me to see her. I made an appointment. The day came and I waited anxiously for my turn. In my feeble attempt for validity, I brought along an old group picture of eleven women, including my mom, when she was 18 years old. The picture was taken outside the Lipton Tea factory in Hoboken, N.J.

I will never forget Lydia's reply. She smiled softly and said: "That's easy because she's sitting right next to me" and properly picked her out of the photo! She told me that she had passed from a disease that took her breath away. She told me that she saw her working packing things and that there was a lot of dust or powder and that the ventilation was very poor. She saw that my mom and I were very close and did a lot of things together. She even saw that we liked Disney World. I just want to state that after that first visit, I never tested Lydia again! It brought such joy to be able to have the knowledge that my Mom's ok and that we will always be able to connect with one another on this level. Lydia has become my operator to heaven.

For years now, Lydia has advised me on my health, financial events and on family and friends. Lydia even gave me peace when my beloved pet Yukon passed. She saw her with my mother. I believe that on our journey through life we are destined to meet certain people along the way. How glad am I that I had the privilege and good fortune to meet my friend, Lydia Clar.

MH (Dallas Business Executive)

I have been consulting with Lydia Clar for over four years. Each reading has resulted in something of significance for me. The insight I gained from the readings has been very helpful in either making decisions or understanding and accepting certain occurrences in my life.

On two occasions, Lydia Clar immediately described the presence of two people who passed and were significant in my life. In both cases, the "physical" descriptions and the "messages" were clear and meaningful to me. They were very specific messages that required no interpretation on my part. Both were surprises and unexpected "presences". The key to legitimacy for me was the fact that this information came without asking Lydia about either person or even seeking connection with someone who passed. Furthermore, I had no intention of seeking this information when I met with Lydia.

In addition to these situations, Lydia has correctly revealed many future events that have affected me or my family members. In the most recent case, she forewarned me about some difficulties my son would experience in school. At the time, that type of situation seemed to me to be next to impossible to occur. I was skeptical. She even indicated what the "trigger point" would be. As it turned out, I needed to deal with this "crisis" by making a trip to the school. Upon questioning my son, I learned that the "trigger" was exactly what Lydia said it would be. Armed with this knowledge, I was able to deal with the "crisis" in a more proactive way since it was less shocking to me.

Currently, I am experiencing the unfolding of another event foretold by Lydia. She saw that I would "walk away" from my current job during the summer months. At the time, while I was interested in changing jobs I did not discuss this with her and there were absolutely no prospects for a new job. Today, I am the leading candidate for two different positions that need to be filled before the end of the summer. This prediction was three months before contact with the new companies was even made.

These are just a few examples of Lydia Clar's gift and my positive experiences as a result. Over the years, I have found her readings to be very effective predictions of future events in my life.

YA (Financial Specialist)

For the past five years I have had readings with Lydia Clar. She is one of the best mediums that continually maintain a high level of communication yielding spectacular validating information. Her words do ring true and brings me ultimate uplifting.

In times of uncertainty I have gained clear perspective on the choices I make in my life. I sincerely thank her for being one of the guiding forces in my life.

LV (University Administration)

I met Lydia Clar in the Fall of 2000. My husband of 33 years suffered a fatal heart attack, while we were eating dinner, in the Spring of 1999. It was the most horrifying and shocking thing that I have ever witnessed. I do, however, take comfort in the fact that I was there and he was not alone. I thank God for that. I was terrified and beside myself. I wondered how could this happen? We were so much in love. Of course, I always thought that he would never cross over since we were together for so much of our life. I met my husband when I was 11 and he was 12. We were neighbors, soul mates and high school sweethearts. We just knew that we would get married and be together till the end; which we did. We had 2 great children and we were so happy and so blessed. He was my right hand, a wonderful person, wonderful husband and great father. I would not allow myself to think of life without him and when he passed I was so lost. I started reading every book that I could find on grief and mediums but I was so torn up with my grief and was such an emotional wreck that nothing helped.

One day I picked up a book called "Crossing Over" by John Edward. He mentioned how Lydia Clar had guided him, and how she said to him that one day he was going to be a great medium and that he would help lots of people. I was fascinated. I had this overwhelming desire to meet her. At the end of the book I found her name and phone number. I just had this nagging feeling to call her to ask if she could see me. I decided to call and, to my surprise, and not expecting to hear from her, I was shocked when she answered the phone and made an appointment for me to meet with her. I was elated. I couldn't wait to meet with her. When the day arrived, I was very nervous and anxious. When I met with her she put me at ease and she just made me feel like I had known her for a while. I was astonished on how keen she was. She meditated and asked me who this wonderful man that had crossed over was. She said that he was holding his heart like he had a heart attack – which he had. She went on to describe him just as he was, including the clothes he was wearing.

She surprised me next, by saying that he was showing her our house and the sofa where we always sat together. She said that he was telling her that I felt alone but that he was there sitting right next to me, holding my hand. There were times when I would close my eyes and picture him there. She specifically asked me about the black leather sofa and I said yes, my sofa is black leather, and then she proceeded to inform me that he wanted me to get rid of it because it was depressing me, which was true. I was really amazed by all of this because she had never been to my house. How did she know about my sofa?

Lydia then said that he was telling her to tell me that he was fine and very happy. He said he had finished what he had come to do, that he was still around me and my children and that he loved us.

It is now six years since my husband passed and I remember those terrifying days. I found so much comfort in Lydia's readings and her kindness. She helped me understand a lot about crossing over. My thoughts were: how could I go on if I don't know where he is, how he feels, how he's doing, or whether he was still in pain. Those questions, alone, drove me crazy. Lydia's reading, however, and her contact with him (which let me know that he was ok and that he wasn't in any pain) helped me a great deal. Today, I can write about it and I can even listen to the tapes of the readings and be at peace. She has a wonderful gift and I am forever grateful to her. Thank you Lydia; you are forever in my heart.

P.S. I think the nagging feeling I got in the beginning was my husband sending me to her, because he knew that she is one of the best.

JS (Interior Design Sales)

I had my first reading with Lydia in March of 2001. My soul mate, Mikey had just passed away in January of that year. I was very confused and grieving at that time. My reading gave me a direction and the only peace I had felt in a long time. Without my saying anything to her she read the cards and told me she saw a man diving off a bridge, she also saw a man with a hat leading me to a place that would be special and that I should follow him. Later, after piecing it together, I realized that the man diving off the bridge was Mikey's ashes being sent over the Reception Pass Bridge, in Washington State, where he wanted me to take him. It was confirmation for me and 13 of his family members and friends that went there. It was an amazing trip. On the way back to the airport, I was riding with friends of mine, a husband and wife, whom mike loved very much. Bob, the driver decided to stop at an Oregon State park on the way, even though we didn't have much time left. We walked and hiked up to a waterfall and I stayed back because I was tired. Bob, however, kept calling me to come up to the top. Once I reached the top there was a magnificent waterfall and a railing that was made up of a large log. This log had "Mikey" carved into it. I was so amazed. When I looked at Bob, I realized he was wearing a baseball cap. I told them all what Lydia had said during her reading and they were all changed by the experience. Mikey continues to contact me through Lydia and it is such a wonderful gift.

At another reading, when I was anticipating selling my house and buying another smaller place, Lydia described the home I am in now. She kept seeing a gate on the right side even though the model I wanted only had a gate on the left. Well, after bidding on a few lots and none of them came through I had my realtor check on another one that we saw. In the whole project, this was the only one with the model I wanted that had the gate on the right side!!! We bid on it, I bought it and am very happy here.

At that time, Lydia also told me I would fall in love again and it would be with someone I already knew. I was very lonely and sad and never thought that could happen to me. About a year and a half later, I had begun to go out and meet people again, but no one appealed to me in that way. One night I ran into an old friend who used to be friends with my first husband. He and his ex-wife had been a part of our old neighborhood, our kids had played ball and we always attended social events where we danced together.

Since that meeting we have been together. We are a great match – as they say made in heaven.

Lydia has guided me and connected me with the true part of my spirit. Her gift truly amazes me all the time. She has been the phone call I receive after a death in the family when there was no way that she could have known about it. Meeting Lydia and attending her readings has brought me the only comfort I have had during the darkest times of my life. That connection is a very powerful one and even if sometimes we don't receive the answers we want, the truth does set us free. I could go on and on with many other answers I have been given. For example, my mother's passing, which is imminent, no longer scares me.

CD (Resides in Canada)

It's hard to remember how many years I have been in contact with Lydia Clar for readings. Although I have never met her face to face, I feel as if she were a sister. A sister, who is much wiser than I am and whom I consult for wisdom and guidance. From the very first PHONE READING she has shown an amazing and accurate insight into my entire family.

I remember when my daughter was pregnant and was due around Christmas, the entire family was absolutely certain that she was having another girl. The day before she was going into the doctor's office for an ultrasound to find out the sex of the baby, I had a reading with Lydia. She asked if we were aware that the baby was a boy and that he would be born closer to the first 2 weeks in December due to complications. I accompanied my daughter to the doctor's office and nearly fell off the stool when the doctor announced first, that she was having a boy and then, repeated nearly word-for-word what I had earlier heard from Lydia about them wanting to induce labor in the first week of December.

Every time that we talked she would ask about the person who had a heart problem and high blood pressure. I would guess that I thought it was my daughter because at one time she had had a heart murmur. Lydia, however, would always insist that it wasn't her. It never occurred to me that she was picking up on my ex-husband who was the father to my children. After two years of expressing concern over the person who had the heart and blood pressure problems, I finally realized who it was when I was notified that he was taking an early retirement due to his heart and blood pressure problems. Without wanting to alarm him, I questioned him one day about his health and he informed me that he had experienced a number of heart attacks and that his blood pressure was at such a dangerous level that he was forced to retire at age 52. Sadly, he passed away a few months later due to a number of debilitating strokes.

I was in the process of selling my house when I had another reading. Lydia informed me that the house would sell for the asking price but that there would be a problem that would delay the closing for about one week. It won't affect the sale of the house; the closing would just be delayed. Two days prior to the scheduled closing date, the pool pump went out. I thought, oh no, I'll bet this must be it. I'll get this fixed and close as scheduled. I had the part needed sent overnight and was feeling smug that I had thwarted her prediction. The morning of the closing I received a phone call from the lawyer's office telling me that the closing was delayed. It was something to do with a problem between the buyers and the mortgage company they were using. A week and a half later, the closing proceeded without a hitch.

I have really learned the hard way that when Lydia gives me a heads up about an impending problem I have to listen. She told me that I was going to have to be firm and not feel pressured into making a decision that was coming up. Boy, am I ever sorry that I didn't heed her advice. I allowed my son to badger and pressure me into lending him a substantial amount of money; actually it was the entire profit from the sale of my house. Two years later, he has still not paid me any of it back. That money was our total savings and today that decision prevents me from moving away from my present location, as I want to do.

Lydia has been right concerning other personal, health, and legal issues. While some of them didn't make sense to me right away and didn't come into fruition until later, when she did put a time line on it, it usually occurred within that time frame.

My current husband was working in Afghanistan and loved working there. In my next reading (2005), Lydia said that something was going to change with his job, that he wasn't going to stay there, he wouldn't be involved in doing the same thing and that he wasn't going to be very happy about it. I informed my husband about the reading and he kind of scoffed at the idea since he was so comfortable and felt his job and location were secure. Two days later, he e-mailed me that there had been a conflict with a co-worker, that he was quitting where he was and that he wanted to work with another agency in another part of Afghanistan. We thought: could this be what Lydia was referring to? We got our answer a week later. Within that week the conflict with the co-worker had been handled and he was back to his job. A few weeks after that, however, my husband called and said that he was being deployed to the Sudan, that his responsibilities would be hands-on and not supervisory (as his present assignment was) and that his living arrangements would be less than what he had in Afghanistan.

I keep some of Lydia's other prediction, not yet confirmed, tucked back away in my mind and wait for them to occur.

I have been to many other people who call themselves psychics and I wasted a whole lot of money. Lydia is so accurate and right on, that there is no need to try anyone else. I feel her warmth connecting every time we talk. For me, it like she's known me my entire life and is either a good friend or sister who I go to for guidance and direction.

Lydia has connected with my mother, who has passed, and given me the comfort and feeling of love that my mother was sending to me. I believe that since having been associated with Lydia and using her meditation tape, that I have become much more acutely aware of the signs that are around me and have learned to acknowledge them more frequently. Lydia has helped me heal relationships both with those who have passed and those in my present life. Her insight into upcoming events is so phenomenal that getting a reading from her is like receiving a gift that I get to open before anyone else does. May God Bless her.

DZ (Teacher)

On November 2, 2002, I started getting readings from Lydia. I was at a crossroad in my life. I was in a bad marriage, had small children and had just gone back to school to finish my degree. Lydia's readings were very comforting. She picked up on my parents (both deceased), described them in a way that I could confirm, and she told me they were looking out for me.

I was thinking about moving out of my immediate area at that time, but Lydia saw job opportunities close by and suggested that a move would not be in my best interest. I did find a job in January, the month that Lydia said it would happen. I was also worried about child care and once again, Lydia assured me that a neighbor would help me, and she did!

Lydia also told me about a woman with "reddish hair" who would be very significant in my life. I have since met her and she has become my best friend and guardian angel. I feel that I am at a better place now because of Lydia's guidance.

BL (Educator)

I have known and scheduled phone consultations with Lydia Clar since December 16, 2002. I have found her readings to be accurate in predicting future personal events. Her guidance and wisdom have supported and prepared me for many life experiences.

Lydia's readings are straight forward and unbelievably accurate. She has foretold of events that came to pass and spoke about feelings I had not discussed with anyone, besides my deceased grandmother.

I am not sure how Lydia is able to gather such accurate information, but I am thankful for her abilities. Her kindness and truthfulness are greatly appreciated.

SC (Medical Office Manager)

I have known Lydia Clar for approximately three years and had my first reading with her on the recommendation of my best friend. My father, whom I was extremely close to, had passed away. I missed him on a daily basis.

At first, I was very skeptical, but after spending an hour with Lydia my feelings that special people have special gifts were confirmed. Lydia Clar is one of them. She told me about situations and events that only I would know about my Dad. The reading did progress to areas about me, my son and family. I must say that Lydia has been 100% insightful and has helped and guided me. She creates a warm and mutually responsive reading.

I have continued to go for an annual reading since that time.

MB (Taken From Client Letter/Canada)

Dear Lydia:

I likely need to re-introduce myself to you, and even then, I'm sure you may not even remember, as I can't begin to imagine the number of people you have crossed paths with. Still, I feel compelled to write this letter to you to express my thanks and gratitude for a telephone reading you conducted with me on August 4, 2004.

I don't even know where to begin Lydia, and if I tried to relay all the events of the past months this would be a very lengthy letter. You relayed that you saw a possible move for us in either December 2004 or January 2005, that you saw my husband signing some papers and that it would be very good for us. Well, last Fall, a headhunter called my husband and he accepted a position with a new company near Calgary, Alberta, Canada (we were living in Lloydminster, Alberta). He moved to begin his new job in January of 2005. I followed with our family this April. This was a very big decision for us as my husband had been with the same company for 13 years and they informed him of a pending move to Illinois this coming summer. In my reading you mentioned it would be alright if we didn't move in December/January but it would be very good for us if we did. This helped us make one of our biggest family decisions in recent memory. The day we were to make our final decision, I received your Christmas greetings letter in the mail. I firmly believe everything happens for a reason and this was a gentle reminder to trust. We were given the gift of confidence that this path we have chosen was the best path for our family. Our move and transition period has been progressing remarkably well. I have many times given thanks for the blessing of having found you and thanks to God for the gifts he has bestowed on you. I have even asked your angels to let you know the appreciation I feel and, of course, to let mine know how much I appreciated their participation in the process.

There were many other aspects of my reading that were tremendously meaningful to me and it is an experience that will live with me forever. Many insights I received from the reading have manifested themselves in truths. I hope to fulfill my spiritual purpose on this earth to the best of my abilities and although I sometimes stray from the path, I'm sure I have never felt more certain that I am on an exciting journey. My finding you was certainly no accident and I will be always grateful.

I hope this letter finds you well and may God Bless. Sincerely, MB

CW (Business Owner)

Rarely have I had a reading with Lydia Clar that has not been correct. She is an amazingly gifted and talented woman. I've turned to Lydia many times in the past several years for advice and though I've argued with her at times when I thought she might be incorrect, she has consistently proved me wrong. God has truly blessed her with an incredible insight and intuition. Following are a few situations from my readings to confirm my statement:

1. When Lydia did my first reading, she said there was a blond haired, blue eyed man around my work who loved me. That description, to my knowledge, didn't fit anyone I worked with so I disagreed with her, but she remained firm in her conviction. She continued to predict this for two years. To my surprise, two years later, a 26 year old field crew member who worked with the construction company I worked with, came to my office door and finally confided in me that he'd had a horrible crush on me since the day I started working there two years earlier. He'd been afraid to ask me out. I dated him once after that and although it never went anywhere, she was absolutely correct in her descriptions of him and his feelings toward me.

2. Later, while working for a company I was unhappy with, Lydia told me I'd be moving on to a job that I could be doing out of my home. She said it would be similar to something I used to do before and it would be perfect for me. One year later, after I'd lost the job about which Lydia had given me that reading, I found another job, am working from my home, doing what I used to do at the company I was working at and doing the same type of work. I am not only still working at this job, from my home as she said, but earning all of the money she told me I'd earn. It's a perfect fit for me and my family.

3. Lydia told me she saw my father signing legal documents for property of some kind which would be for me. She saw this in two readings. In October 2004, my father signed legal documents to give me a car as a gift.

4. When Lydia talked about my youngest son, Garrett, she mentioned that he had back problems that started from a bad fall. She said my older son and I needed to really push him to do his back exercises, otherwise, his

back problems would continue to worsen. This was all totally correct and very startling since I'd never mentioned Garrett's fall from his bicycle, which caused a large lump to form on his upper back. I'd taken him to physical therapy but the only way I could get him to do his exercises was to continually harp on him.

5. For the past three years Lydia has predicted that there would be an issue involving my ex-husband, the sale of my house and money he wanted from me. This prediction has occurred with every reading, causing me to worry about the loss of my home. Recently though, I have earned all the money Lydia had correctly predicted I'd earn with my new job and will soon have all the necessary money needed to completely pay off the equity I owe my ex-husband on the house I won in the divorce settlement. Once that's paid off, the house is mine free and clear. The lien will be released and I will no longer have to live in fear of his forcing me and my children out of our home.

6. When Lydia first mentioned my deceased Grandmother, she said she could identify her by the phrase I say to people to describe her, "she was just like a Mother to me." No one but me and a few individuals would have any knowledge of that phrase, especially Lydia, since I'd never mentioned my Grandmother to her before. At that moment I was a true believer in Lydia's gift.

LYDIA'S VALIDATION
TO JOHN EDWARD

John Edward is a gifted medium, author and host of the television shows *Crossing Over* AND *Cross Country*. John has continuously validated my efforts in starting him on his own path of development. Now I want to take this opportunity to validate HIS talent. It is through his own hard work, persistence and determination, despite some very trying situations, that John has succeeded.

Today, he is a shining light in a world where many are filled with darkness and despair. He offers spiritual awakening and relief to those whose loved ones have passed over.

In my opinion, he is part of a greater universal plan to disseminate knowledge about spirit and spirituality in a more positive and enlightened way. He gives hope to those in personal turmoil and those searching for answers.

His books, seminars and televisions appearances encourage people around the world to develop their own abilities and has brought worldwide recognition and acceptance of the spiritual world.

John, I salute you – great job!

CONCLUSION

"History" is ever changing and each one of us forms a small part of that history. What we know now, is like the iceberg, only the tip shows while 80% is below the surface. In the paranormal field, like science, new things are being discovered all of the time and yesterday's mysteries become today's realities.

As new insights emerge, understanding and application lead to still higher truths and the search is constantly renewed. Each discovery opens new doors that invite us to delve further. I hope this book creates the desire for further investigation into whatever area of study you choose.

Those of us who choose to look ahead and continue to learn, should bear in mind the observation of Arthur C. Clark, the science fiction writer who said: "The further advanced a civilization, the closer it seems to magic."